Day by Day:
Professional Journaling for Library Media Specialists

Donna Miller
Karen Larsen

Library of Congress Cataloging-in-Publication Data

Miller, Donna P., 1948-
  Day by day : professional journaling for library media specialists /
by Donna Miller and Karen Larsen.
     p. cm.
Includes bibliographical references.
  ISBN 1-58683-087-2
  1. School librarians--Diaries. 2. Diaries--Authorship. I. Larsen,
Karen, 1958- II. Title.
  Z682.4.S34M55 2003
  027.8--dc21
                                2003011717

Published by Linworth Publishing, Inc.
480 East Wilson Bridge Road, Suite L
Worthington, Ohio 43085

Copyright © 2003 by Linworth Publishing, Inc.

All rights reserved. Purchasing this book entitles a librarian to reproduce activity sheets for use in the library within a school or entitles a teacher to reproduce activity sheets for single classroom use within a school. Other portions of the book (up to 15 pages) may be copied for staff development purposes within a single school. Standard citation information should appear on each page. The reproduction of any part of this book for an entire school or school system or for commercial use is strictly prohibited. No part of this book may be electronically reproduced, transmitted or recorded without written permission from the publisher.

ISBN: 1-58683-087-2

5 4 3 2 1

Table of Contents

Dedication iv

Acknowledgements v

Introduction vii

        Protect Your Thoughts: The Importance of Privacy vii
        Format is Fundamental: Types of Journal "Books". viii
        Quill or Cursor: With What Will You Write? viii
        Steps to Start: Preliminary Efforts for Effectiveness. ix
        Diary Devices: Tools to "Jumpstart" Your Writing. x
        So What's in It For Me?" How This Book Can Benefit
        Library Media Specialists. xi

Journal Reflections. xiii

        General Writing Prompts xiii
        January 1
        February 16
        March 31
        April 47
        May. 62
        June. 77
        July 92
        August. 108
        September 123
        October 138
        November 154
        December 169

Bibliography. 185

For Further Reading 185

About the Authors 186

Dedication

To my father Donald Pool who taught me to "get up one more time and try again" and to my mother Patsy Randol who continues to show me that reading and writing truly are balms for the soul.

Donna Miller

I would like to dedicate this book to my father and mother, Henry and Wilma Krueger who always read to me and now read to their granddaughters.

"You may have tangible wealth untold; Caskets of jewels and coffers of gold. Richer than I you will never be — I had a mother (and a father) who read to me."
— Strickland Gillilan

Karen Larsen

Acknowledgements

The authors would like to thank Marlene Woo-Lun at Linworth Publishing for giving us the opportunity to share this book with our colleagues. A special thanks also goes to the staff at Linworth for their support and assistance throughout the writing of this book. To our editor Sherry York, we express our gratitude for her wise counsel and kind and consistent encouragement. Finally, to our families we want to express deep affection and appreciation for their continual support, love, and patience as they "kept the home fires burning" throughout our struggles and successes in finding just the right words to express our thoughts and feelings to readers.

Introduction

You may remember keeping a diary when you were younger. Some adults maintain this practice as a tool for reflection, self-improvement, emotional release, recording and preserving the family history, keeping track of important milestones and events, or for other purposes. A journal is similar to a diary, but there are some important differences. According to James E. Miller, a diary is "a day-to-day record of how you spend your time" whereas a journal focuses instead on "the writer's interior life – how you feel about something at the moment, or what you think about some matter that has grabbed your attention." (9) This book deals with a specific type of journal writing, i.e., professional journal writing. Although recording events and emotions will certainly be appropriate, the focus of this type of journal writing is somewhat different from that of personal journal writing.

So what are the differences between professional journaling and personal journaling? The most obvious difference, of course, is that a professional journal is used to record events, emotions, milestones, and other items that relate to one's career. Beyond that, the techniques for writing in a professional journal can be very similar to those used for personal journal writing. Such devices as prompts, questions, reflections, free writing, and others can be used for both types of journals. It is not the medium but the message that differentiates the two types of journals. The book will begin with the common tools, strategies, and devices that apply to all types of journals and then narrow the focus to those items that primarily apply to professional journal writing, with particular emphasis on specific items that are important for library media specialists.

Protect Your Thoughts: The Importance of Privacy

Several rules or suggestions for journal writing are universal. First, a journal contains the private thoughts, ideas, and reflections of the author of the journal. Although journals can be shared if desired, it is typical to keep most of the contents of a journal private. It is especially important in the case of professional journals that the author find a place to keep the journal that facilitates maintaining this privacy. Miller advises that journal writers keep their journals "out of obvious sight" and even perhaps hide or lock them away. (21) While actually locking your journal away may sound extreme, in the case of a professional journal this is very important. In fact, unless the professional journal is to be included as a part of the writer's evaluation portfolio, it might be best to keep the journal away from the work site. As with e-mail messages that are sent, received, and stored at a person's place of work, a journal could be considered to be the property of the business place at which it is kept, in the case of library media specialists, the school or district for which one works. If the journal entries include sensitive information — especially entries in which the writer expresses negative thoughts, feelings, or opinions about administrators, teachers, or other staff, it is best to store the journal at home.

Format is Fundamental: Types of Journal "Books"

It is important for writers to decide what type of journal to use. A multitude of formats exists, from a simple notepad to Web-based journals. The various types of journals include such formats as word processors, electronic (Web-based) journals, lined legal pads, unlined pads or paper, spiral notebooks, ring binders, commercially produced journals (such as this one), and even index cards. The list could go on and on, and the writer needs to decide which type works best for him. Each type of journal has advantages and disadvantages, most of which can be ascertained by using simple logic. For example, if the writer wants a journal that can be rearranged from time to time, it is probably best not to use a steno or legal pad. A ring binder or word processor would facilitate editing and rearranging much more effectively. If, on the other hand, the writer wants to store her journal in the bottom of a dresser drawer, a small notepad might work best. If the writer wants a journal that is specifically designed for certain purposes, a journal book directed toward the person's career or hobby might work best. This journal book, for example, includes not only the standard blank daily pages for recording entries, but also tips, reminders, special events, and other items developed to meet the particular needs of school library media specialists. The authors have attempted to make this journal practical and valuable for their peers and welcome any suggestions for subsequent editions of this book to make it more librarian-friendly.

Quill or Cursor: With What Will You Write?

Do you have a favorite pen, pencil, marker, or other writing utensil? If so, you probably realize how important using just the right writing instrument can be – especially for those of us who are kinesthetically oriented. For permanence, ink is usually better than pencil lead if the writer intends for the journal to last for a long time. However, since a professional journal does not typically cover the entire span of a person's life, a pencil might be acceptable for recording the entries. Once the writer becomes dedicated to the practice of writing in a professional journal, the importance of using a comfortable writing utensil will become apparent. Just like breaking in new shoes, it is helpful to "practice" with your pen or pencil for a bit before using it for your journal writing.

Steps to Start: Preliminary Efforts for Effectiveness

1) Determine your purpose.

With a personal journal, it is not critical that the writer have a specific purpose for writing in mind. Mere catharsis may be the only reason one writes. This is not true with a professional journal. In fact, having a purpose may be the single most important factor in successful professional journal writing. It is one's purpose that serves as a catalyst for the writer to continue making entries, and the purpose will assist the writer in maintaining a focus so that the journal is a productive and beneficial tool. As with the types of journals available, the purposes for writing in a professional journal are numerous. These purposes can include but are not limited to:

- Time management
- Assessing strengths and weaknesses
- Goal setting
- CYA tool (cover your anatomy)
- Working through professional problems/situations
- Analyzing and improving relationships with co-workers or supervisors
- Identifying "what went wrong" in professional situations
- Identifying successful practice with the purpose of replicating it
- Professional growth
- Getting published
- Combinations of the above
- Others

When the writer experiences "writer's block" or is unable to write a cogent entry in the professional journal, re-visiting his/her purpose can help the writer re-focus and begin writing again.

2) Find a suitable place to write.

Just as the location for storing the professional journal is important, so is the location for writing in the journal. Obviously trying to write in your journal in the midst of the library media center when noisy students are around is not feasible. Since privacy is important, it might be best to make journal entries at home. However, sometimes it is best to capture at least the essence of an event immediately following it, so writers may want to jot down brief impressions, thoughts, and feelings about the event while at work and then "flesh out" the journal entry later at home.

In addition to deciding upon a physical location, such features as lighting, furnishings, colors, and décor can be important. If writers need to feel calm and rested when they write, a room with vivid yellow walls and fluorescent lighting might not be the best choice. On the other hand, if the writer wants to feel energized when recording a successful situation, a colorful room might be perfect! Deciding upon a place to write means not only finding a place that is comfortable but going a bit farther perhaps to find a place that inspires the writer to journal about a specific type of situation or event.

3) Determine the best time to write.

The time of day for writing is as individual as are the writers of journals. Some people are "morning persons" and others are "night owls," so it is important that each person decide what time of day or evening works best for her. Of course, it may not always be possible to write in the journal at the optimum time of day due to the pressures of family, household chores, community or church obligations, or other factors, but as much as is possible, it is advantageous for writers to select a time during which they are most productive. It is, in fact, a good practice to "schedule" your writing and make it a priority. The important factor in forming any type of habit is practicing the behavior regularly and consistently. Journal writing definitely needs to become a habit if writers are to use this tool effectively — especially professional journal writing.

4) Be as comfortable as possible when writing in your journal.

Tight, restrictive clothes, extreme heat or cold, loud noises, uncomfortable chairs, and other factors can negatively impact journal writing. Although this may seem apparent, it is sometimes tempting to simply find the nearest corner in which to sit and begin writing — especially if the writer is using the journal for catharsis. While one may be able to pour out one's professional soul in a cramped chair situated in a dark corner, this is not the optimum situation for performing purposeful, thoughtful analysis and problem solving. Thus, it is more effective to take the time to be comfortable and relaxed so that the entries can truly be useful in fulfilling one's purpose for writing.

5) Just write!

This edict is not always easy, but if all the writer does is simply write whatever words come to mind in an effort to begin the journaling process, that is better than trying to find just the right words to describe an event, develop a goal, or express the exact feeling that was experienced in a professional situation. Using some writing devices as described below to jumpstart your writing will eventually result in the writer being able to more easily capture the specific words and feelings experienced in order to fulfill the writing goal for the day or for a writing session.

Diary Devices:
Tools to Jumpstart Your Writing

Sometimes sentences, phrases, or words such as those included in the General Writing Prompts section of this book can be used as catalysts when the proverbial writer's block occurs. Barbara Woodard includes a lengthy list of these types of sentences in her book *Journal Jumpstarts: Quick Topics and Tips for Journal Writing*. Although her book is written to be used with students, some of these prompts such as "Who are you — really?" and "What is the greatest lesson you have ever learned?" are generic enough to be beneficial for all journal authors, including those writing a professional journal. (19) In fact, for novice journal writers, having a variety of tools available can definitely make getting started with the writing process much smoother and help writers to write more effectively.

In her book *The New Diary: How to Use a Journal for Self Guidance and Expanded Creativity*, Tristine Rainer provides a list of devices to bring awareness to journal writers of "the range of ways to write in a diary." (52) These devices include:

- Catharsis
- Description
- Free-Intuitive Writing
- Reflection
- List
- Portrait
- Map of Consciousness
- Guided Imagery
- Altered Point of View
- Unsent Letter
- Dialogue

Rainer describes each of the above thoroughly and tells writers how to use them. Although some are not necessarily appropriate for professional journaling, most of these devices can serve as helpful tools for professional journal writers and should, therefore, be incorporated whenever writing becomes difficult or to fulfill a specific purpose. For example, a writer could use a list when he is developing goals by listing all of the items in the library program that are important and then writing these as goal statements.

In addition to the above devices, tools such as sentence completion, free association (writing whatever comes to mind), questions, and formal prompts can be used to assist writers in getting words on paper. This book will include some of these tools that are focused specifically on areas pertinent to and relevant for library media specialists.

So What's In It For Me? How This Book Can Benefit Library Media Specialists

This book differs from other journals in that it is designed to meet the professional journaling needs of library media specialists. To that end, scattered throughout the journal pages are helpful hints from the "Tips" and "Shoptalk" columns in *The Book Report* and *Library Talk* magazines, the precursors to Linworth Publishing's *LMC: Library Media Connection* magazine, as well as suggestions by the authors of this book. Also included are journal prompts appropriate for library media specialists; notices about special days, authors' birthdays, and holidays; and finally, humorous and inspirational quotes from a great variety of people. The prompts, tips, reminders of special days, and other items included in the book can be used to help readers plan, set goals, reflect, and improve your practice. Feel free to use the tools in this book as desired, realizing that you can select only the tools that fit your needs and disregard others.

After reading this introductory guide to professional journal writing and starting the exciting and fulfilling journey of beginning your own journal, what is next? How can the journal actually be used to improve practice and promote professional growth? The specific use for your journal again goes back to your purpose. If you want to use your journal to help you maintain a professional portfolio for your annual evaluation, the items in this book can be incorporated into your portfolio as needed to help you remember significant accomplishments, examine your weaker areas so that you can begin to work on them, and articulate your goals to your principal.

Library media specialist Alice Yucht, a well-known presenter and author of *Flip It! An Information Skills Strategy for Student Researchers* uses a simple technique for tracking her communication and collaboration with teachers that could easily be incorporated into a journal. Yucht lists the names of every teacher in her building in a notebook, each on a separate page. Whenever communication occurs between her and the teacher, she writes the date, and then places an arrow in the margin to indicate who initiated the conversation. An arrow pointing out, or left, indicates that the teacher initiated the meeting, and an arrow pointing in, or right, indicates that Alice began the conversation. This quickly shows Alice which teachers are coming to her for resources or services and which ones she has proactively approached. (Yucht n. pag.) A tool like this one would definitely be handy to demonstrate to your principal how frequently the library media center is being used and by whom. Of course, the details of important conversations would be included in the narrative part of your journal as necessary.

If your purpose is to better manage your time, you could use your journal to list the tasks you perform each day with a notation beside each task indicating the time spent. Then you could begin to analyze how you are spending your time and make adjustments as needed. This book provides prompts and questions about various tasks to be completed that can help you identify and track recurring tasks throughout the year.

Library and education publishers are always looking for new authors who can share fresh ideas with colleagues. We library media specialists are usually certified teachers as well as credentialed librarians, so we have much knowledge and experience to contribute. If you are an aspiring writer, use your journal to capture your good ideas and inspirations. The quotes and reminders in this book can serve as catalysts to help you identify these passions and areas of expertise that could provide the basis for a book or magazine article proposal. Getting published is not as daunting as it might seem, and a professional journal can make this process even easier.

A bibliography of works cited and further readings are included at the end of the book for those who want to engage in more in-depth study of journal writing. Included below are some general journal reflections in the form of sentence completions that can also be used as they are needed. Get your paper or computer and pen or keyboard ready, and prepare to embark on an exciting journey – that of writing about your very own experiences in the library field.

*"Thus it is that I have now undertaken, in my eighty-third year, to tell my personal myth. I can only make direct statements, only 'tell stories.' Whether or not the stories are 'true' is not the problem. The only question is whether what I tell is **my** fable, **my** truth."*
—*Carl Jung*

Journal Reflections:

General Writing Prompts:

What if . . .
What do you think . . .
When I . . . then . . .
What . . .
How . . .
Describe . . .
When . . .
Which . . .
Who . . .
Where . . .
Why . . .
Do . . .
The most important thing is . . .
If only I had . . .
Thank goodness I . . .
I was afraid when . . .
The first time I . . .
My greatest fear is . . .
My greatest success is . . .
The worst that can happen is . . .
The best that can happen is . . .
I love . . .
I hate . . .
I wish . . .
I should . . .
In what ways can . .
How do I feel about . . .
What are my feelings about . . .

"It is not often that someone comes along who is a true friend and a good writer. Charlotte was both."
—*E.B. White*

January

> January is here, with eyes that keenly glow,
> A frost-mailed warrior
> striding a shadowy steed of snow.
> — *Edgar Fawcett*

January 1   Happy New Year!

*What three resolutions would you like to keep?

> *"Blasts of January would blow you through and through."*
> — *William Shakespeare*

_____
_____
_____
_____
_____
_____
_____
_____

*Tip: When writing resolutions or goal statements, make sure your goals are smart: **S**pecific, **M**easurable, **A**cceptable, **R**ealistic, **T**ime frame.*

January 2

* What if . . .

> *"The teacher is one who makes two ideas grow where only one grew before."*
> — *Elbert Hubbard*

_____
_____
_____
_____
_____
_____
_____

Tip: I barcode all our library's TVs, VCRs, and their respective remotes. Our barcode labels came with a smaller sticker with the same number. I put the small sticker on the remote and the barcode on the VCR or TV. The TV and CART also each have their own barcode. When a teacher checks out a cart, TV, and VCR, I need to check out three items.
— David Lininger, Library Media Specialist, Hickory County R-1 Schools, Urbana, Missouri
(Library Talk *September/October 2001*)

January 3

* What do you think...would say if I changed...

> "What wild desires, what restless torments seize The hapless man, who feels the book-disease."
> — Dr. John Ferriar, "The Bibliomanic: An Epistle to Richard Herber, Esq.," 1863

Tip: http://www.aclin.org/ is the link to the Colorado Virtual library. When you get there, click on the link for Colorado Kids, Parents & Teachers. This will take you to lesson plans and tons of research links for students doing research. It is free and very easy to use.

January 4   1933   Phyllis Naylor

* When I . . . then . . .

> "From the age of six I have haunted the library... it frightens me to think of what I might have become — and what I might have failed to become — without one."
> — Isaac Asimov

Tip: Attend a state or national library conference to stay current with the latest thinking in your field.

January 5

* The most important thing is . . .

_____

_____

_____

_____

_____

_____

_____

> "In my day the library was a wonderful place... We didn't have visual aids and didn't have various programs... it was a sanctuary... So I tend to think the library should remain a center of knowledge."
> — Cited in American Libraries

Tip: Take your kids camping. Begin by pulling all the books you have on camping, both fiction and nonfiction. Then set up small pop-up tents in a circle. You can bring in any camping gear you may have such as sleeping bags, flashlights, and camp cooking equipment. Ask classroom teachers to help. Dress in jeans and flannel. Read with the lights out and flashlights on. Share your favorite book on camping with your kids.
— Lisa Fuller, Rock Cut Elementary School, Loves Park, Illinois (Library Talk May/June 2001)

January 6   1919   Vera Cleaver
               1878   Carl Sandburg

* Describe a time when you felt successful.

_____

_____

_____

_____

_____

_____

> "Let books be your dining table,
> And you shall be full of delights
> Let them be your mattress
> And you shall sleep restful nights"
> — Quoted in Bar Hebraues' Ethicon
> St. Ephrem the Syrian

Tip: Need an eye-catching bulletin board that promotes all of the many things you do? Try picking up various socks at the local discount store. (I use baby socks, hunter's socks, athletic socks, Winnie the Pooh socks, and Dr. Seuss socks). Hang them on the bulletin board. List your library's services (e.g., online resources, leisure reading, audio books, CD-ROM) on streamers, then position each streamer to come out of the opening of the sock. Underneath, add the caption, "Our library will knock your socks off!"
— Christine Findlay, Centerville (Ohio) City Schools (Library Talk March/April 2001)

January 7

1936 Kay Chorao
1906 Eleanor Clymer
1926 Rosekrans Hoffman

* I can't believe . . .

> "Tis the good reader that makes the good book; a good head cannot read amiss: in every book he finds passages which seem confidences or asides hidden from all else and unmistakably meant for his ear."
> —Ralph Waldo Emerson

Tip: Many stories lend themselves to sound effects. Borrow some instruments from the music teacher and have the students be the sound effects crew.

January 8
Elvis' Birthday! (OK, he never wrote a book, but he is the King!)

*What do you do to give children the feeling that he or she "belongs"?

> "I ain't no saint, but I've tried never to do anything that would hurt my family or offend God . . . I figure all any kid needs is hope and the feeling he or she belongs. If I could do or say anything that would give some kid that feeling, I would believe I had contributed something to the world."
> —Elvis Presley, commenting to a reporter, 1950s

Tip: Take a look at your biographies. These can go out of date rather quickly. Is the information current? Is this book still being checked out? Is the book in good shape? Does the collection represent men and women? Is the collection diverse? Does it fit the instructional needs of the staff?

January 9   1914   Clyde Robert Bulla

*What are you doing that is not working? What changes could be made to make it work? Is this an idea that should be abandoned altogether?

> "Results! Why, man, I have gotten a lot of results. I know several thousand things that won't work."
> —Thomas Edison

Tip: Our school broadcasts school announcements via closed-circuit TV. Every Monday, I recruit a staff member or student to do a short book talk, called Get It, Read It, for this announcement program. This is an easy library promotion to organize and maintain yet it publicizes the IMC collection and demonstrates the "reading" nature of a range of district employees and students.
  —*Valerie Edwards, IMC Director, Montona Grove High School, Montona, Wisconsin*
  (The Book Report November/December 2001)

January 10   1929   Remy Charlip

*Thank goodness I . . .

> "Nutrimentum spiritus."
> (Food for the soul.)
> —Inscription on the Berlin Royal Library.

Tip: Join your state library and reading associations. These groups are invaluable sources of support and information. Attending their conferences will keep you up to date in the library field.

January 11
1918   Robert C. O'Brien
1931   Mary Rodgers

*Imagine a video camera crew followed you around all day today filming a typical day in a librarian's life. What parts would you want them to keep in the final film and what parts would you want them to edit? How would your day be different if you were really filmed all day?

> "Live in such a way that you would not be ashamed to sell your parrot to the town gossip."
> —Will Rogers

_____
_____
_____
_____
_____
_____
_____

Tip: Put a note in your newsletter to parents announcing that you accept donations of gently used books. Those that you don't need for the collection can be passed on to teachers, donated to before and after school programs, or given away as prizes.

January 12
1874   Laura Adams Armer
1908   Clement Hurd
1876   Jack London
1628   Charles Perrault

*Why did . . . . ? What am I going to do about it?

> "There's nothing to match curling up with a good book when there's a repair job to be done around the house."
> —Joe Ryan

_____
_____
_____
_____
_____
_____
_____

Tip:
When collaborating with the classroom teacher on a lesson, invite the art and music teachers in also to see how their areas can incorporate what the children are learning in class.

January 13
1932	Horatio Alger
1926	Michael Bond

*What are you doing that is working? What are you proud of?

_____
_____
_____
_____
_____

Tip: When team teaching a lesson or project with teachers, ask them to suggest a topic. Write up a bibliography and possible project/paper plans for them to use. Refine them together and make notes of what works and what doesn't. Keep copies of the bibliographies, teaching tools, and handouts in a 3-ring binder labeled by year. That way, when the teachers come back frantically the next year and ask, "What was that project we did on the Revolution?" you can pull it out. This process is also handy for children who lose their material. I find filing projects by date rather than by teacher is preferable as units are usually done in the same order each year.
—Anne Shiply, Waterloo, New York, (Library Talk September/October 2000)

January 14
1874	Thornton Burgess
1886	Hugh Lofting
1943	Pat R. Mauser
1882	Hendrick W. van Loon

*Who are your most supportive parents? What do they do that enhances the library program? How can you include other parents in this group to build advocacy for your library program?

> *"There is not such a cradle of democracy upon the earth as the Free Public Library, this republic of letters, where neither rank, office, nor wealth receives the slightest consideration."*
> —*Andrew Carnegie*

_____
_____
_____

Tip: Fantasy books are frequently written in a series. Because we witnessed a dramatic increase in fantasy reading, I devised a system to help the students read the books in order. I wrote the number of the series on the top of the book. For example, on The Great Hunt by Robert Jordan I wrote the number "2." Now the students can see at a glance which book comes next.
—Eileen B. Jones, Hillcrest High School, Simpsonville, South Carolina (The Book Report September/October 2002)

January 15

*The most successful encounter I had today was . . .
It helped me grow professionally by . . .

> "Learn to pause . . . or nothing worthwhile will catch up to you."
> —Don King

_____
_____
_____
_____
_____
_____
_____
_____

Tip: To help you easily find out what you have in all of the storage containers, type up what's in each box and place the list in a Fed Ex envelope (the clear adhesive kind), and stick it to the front of the container so you don't have to lift all the lids to see what's in a box.

January 16

* Just once, I would like to . . .

> "It's one thing to be in a bookstore. But to see your book in a library, to me that really means something."
> —David Sedaris (Public Libraries *interview*)

_____
_____
_____
_____
_____
_____

Tip: Ever had a teacher stop you in the hall, the office, or during lunch and ask you to do this or that? Maybe they tell you they need a video or a bulb. You hear yourself say, "Sure," as you smile and wonder, "How will I remember that?" If you wear a watch, move it from one wrist to the other. Think about what you need to remember while moving the watch. Do not let yourself move the watch back to its normal and more comfortable spot until you have handled the request.

—Debra Kay Logan, Taft Middle School, Marion, Ohio, The Book Report January/February 2001)

January 17 1938   John C. Bellairs
               1925   Robert Cormier

> *"Where is human nature so weak as in the bookstore!"*
> —Henry Ward Beecher,
> Star Papers; or Experiences
> of Art and Nature, *1855*

*What are my feelings about . . .

___

___

___

___

___

___

___

Tip: Use white "Christmas" lights to outline your bulletin board that you have covered with black paper. Put the caption "Now Showing" at the top of the bulletin board in white letters. Place a photo or the name of an author on the bulletin board with jackets from his/her books scattered around the bulletin. This display can be changed every week to highlight different authors. Plug in the lights, and voila! Instant marquee!

January 18 1882   A. A. Milne
               1884   Arthur Ransome

* The first time I taught this unit,
I learned. . .

___

___

___

___

___

___

___

___

Tip: Don't waste time feeling guilty about what you didn't do. It's gone now; move ahead.

January 19
1925 Nina Bawden
1809 Edgar Allan Poe

*What are the strengths and weakness with the technology in your program? What needs immediate attention? What can you showcase?

> "An encyclopedia is a system for collecting dust in alphabetical order."
> —Mike Barfield

_____
_____
_____
_____
_____
_____
_____

Tip: When you need to remember to bring something from home for the next day and you think of it while you are at work, call your home answering machine and leave yourself a message. Conversely, when you are home, you can call your voice mail at work and remind yourself about something for the next day.

January 20
1910 Joy Adamson

*My greatest fear is . . .

> "Today a reader, tomorrow a leader."
> —W. Fusselman

_____
_____
_____
_____
_____
_____
_____

Tip: I put half of a velcro strip on the bottom of our television remote controls and the other half on the bottom of the shelf holding the TV so that it's hardly visible when attached. This system really helps keep the remotes from "walking away."
—Dawne Wheeler Reed, Hohokam Middle School, Tucson, Arizona (Library Talk September/October 2001)

January 21 Martin Luther King Jr.'s birthday

*How are you great? How do you serve?

_____
_____
_____
_____
_____
_____
_____
_____
_____

> "Everybody can be great. Because anybody can serve. You don't have to have a college degree to serve. You don't have to make your subject and your verb agree to serve... You only need a heart full of grace... A soul generated by love."
> —Martin Luther King, Jr. (1919–1968)

Tip: Frequently ask yourself: "What is the best use of my time right now?"

January 22
1930 Blair Lent
1930 Brian Wildsmith

*What color makes you think of happiness? How can you get more of this color into your library?

_____
_____
_____
_____
_____
_____
_____
_____

> "When you read a classic you do not see in the book more than you did before. You see more in you than there was before."
> —Clifton Fadiman

Tip: Laminate a "Cheat Sheet" of the basic bibliography formats. Make them brightly colored and easy to find, or leave them next to computers for quick reference. Kids will come to depend on them.
—Kathy Fritts, Jesuit High School, Portland, Oregon (The Book Report March/April 2000)

Journal Pages 11

January 23

*How can you be a better advocate for libraries? At a school level? Community level? State level? National level?

> *"You know you've read a good book when you turn the last page and feel a little as if you have lost a friend."*
> —Paul Sweeney

___

Tip: For cleaning the "gooky gunk" that accumulates on computer keyboards made by the use of many fingers, use:
1) Alcohol on Q-tips 2) Windex ™ on a paper towel or sponge 3) Baby-wipes 4) The dishwasher! (definitely for MACs, maybe for PCs) Check the manufacturer recommendations prior to trying any of these suggestions.
    *—Cindy Braun, Big Sky and Sentinel High Schools, Missoula, Montana (***Library Talk*** *November/December 2000)*

January 24   1922   John Beatty

*My greatest success is . . .

> *"I've never known any trouble that an hour's reading didn't assuage."*
> —Charles de Secondat

___

Tip: If you're finding your busy teachers don't read your newsletters filled with new titles and media information or come to see the latest display of new books, why not take the new titles to them? Our teachers like receiving "Preview Packs" of new books as they come in. We select books fitting their courses and interests and check them out for them. A media assistant hand delivers them to each teacher. Also, by going to classrooms, reading and booktalking new books, we entice the students to come and see what's new at the media center. So, if your teachers and students won't come to you, go to them!
    *—Gay Ann Loesch, Independence High School, Charlotte, North Carolina (***The Book Report*** *November/December 2000)*

12 Day by Day: Professional Journaling for Library Media Specialists

January 25
1759 Robert Burns
1914 Flora James

*I am the most productive when . . .
I am least productive when . . .

> "Education . . . has produced a vast population able to read but unable to distinguish what is worth reading."
> —Trevelyan

_____
_____
_____
_____
_____

Tip: Our catalog software allows us to include photographs of the items in the records, so we plan to include digital photographs of some of our kits. Once upgraded to the latest version of our software, we will use the 856 tag to include photos of items within a catalog record. To see our test project, go to <sisnet.ssku.k12.ca.us/~imcftp> and choose link #9, "Lending Library Photos."
—Kathy Graves, Siskiyou County Office of Education, Yreka, California (The Book Report March/April 2002)

January 26
1831 Mary Mapes Dodge

*What would happen if children ruled the library? What changes would they make?

> "Too often we give our children answers to remember rather than problems to solve."
> —Roger Lewin

_____
_____
_____
_____
_____
_____

Tip: To get children reading, invite students to share articles from magazines. Participants can have their names published in the monthly school newsletter.
—Madeleine Hoss, Metcalf Laboratory School, Normal, Illinois, (Library Talk January/February 2001)

January 27 1832 Lewis Carroll
1923 Jean Merrill
1928 Harry Allard

> *"Libraries are really about connection, not collections."*
> —Gary Hartzell

*What does this quote mean to you? What connections are made in your library?

_____
_____
_____
_____
_____

    Tip: Students who wish to visit the library at lunchtime sign a sheet that includes their name and the purpose for the visit. Students who leave may reenter with permission only. Those who truly want to take advantage of the library's collection and services appreciate this policy. They can read, work, or browse without being disturbed by groups wandering in to "check out the scene," socialize, or cause disturbances. We now spend less time supervising and more time assisting.
    —Vickie Rabourn, Los Osos (California) Middle School, (The Book Report *January/February 2002*)

January 28

*What are your professional goals for next year? What is your plan for accomplishing them?

> *"Bibliomaniac: A victim of the obsessive-compulsive neurosis characterized by a congested library and an atrophied bank account."*
> —Michael Dunbar, Hooked on Books, *1997*

_____
_____
_____
_____
_____
_____
_____
_____

January 29
1915 Bill Peet
1943 Rosemary Wells

*Nordstom Department Stores™ have found a successful niche in the retail clothing market by providing exemplary customer service. How do you provide quality customer service? Who are all of your "customers," both internal and external? What can you do to make your customer service exemplary?

> "What a school thinks about its library is a measure of what it thinks about education."
> —Harold Howe, former U.S. Commissioner of Education

_____

_____

_____

_____

_____

Tip: Consider having your work desk near the center of the library instead of in a closed office. You will be right in the thick of things and be accessible to students and staff. Save the office for confidential needs such as phone calls and staff reviews.

January 30
1924 Lloyd Alexander

*The worst that can happen is . . .

> "A new library is like finding a $100 bill on the sidewalk."
> —Anonymous library patron
> (As quoted in PUBLIB message, 11 September 2000)

_____

_____

_____

_____

Tip: With over 2,200 students at our school, lunch was a zoo my first year. Now we have a "No Problem!" lunchtime by creating zones for different activities. As they enter, those wanting to read current periodicals slip into an easy chair with a newspaper or a magazine. To their right is a zone for the sociable crowds where the "lunch bunch" talks, tutors, plays chess, or exchanges ideas with friends. In this zone, noise is not an issue; it's okay. To the left of the reading area is a zone filled with electronic resources, the Internet, and a typing area. These folks are so engrossed with computers, it is relatively quiet. Beside this area is a quiet zone where students can do serious research, study, and homework without distractions. After a few weeks of directions, the young people gravitate to the area they need. We make everyone happy from the chatterboxes to the studious.
—Gay Ann Loesch, Independence High School, Charlotte, North Carolina (The Book Report November/December 2000)

February

***February is* I Love To Read Month**
Presidents' Day is in February

Monthly Tip: Chinese New Year falls in either January or February (It changes each year). Find out when the date falls this year. Give away a penny in a small red envelope (make them out of red construction paper and staple them shut) to each person who checks out a book today.

Chinese New Year starts with the New Moon on the first day of the new year and ends on the full moon 15 days later. The 15th day of the New Year is called the Lantern Festival, which is celebrated at night with lantern displays and children carrying lanterns in a parade.

February 1
1902   Langston Hughes
1941   Jerry Spinelli

> *"One of the troubles of the day, observes Mr. C.N. Peac, is that once we came upon the little red schoolhouse, whereas now we come upon the little-read school boy."*
> —Bennet Cerf

Tip: When filling out postcards or writing letters or e-mail to request information, flyers, pamphlets, posters, or other materials from agencies or organizations that send out such items, I always list my name as "Pam File." When the materials come in the mail addressed to that name, I know immediately that the item was requested specifically for my vertical or pamphlet file. It saves time: I can put those items in a pile to process all together at a later time.
—Anna Hartle, Cincinnati (Ohio) Country Day School (Library Talk *May/June 2001*)

February 2 Groundhog Day
1899   Rebecca Caudill
1931   Judith Viorst

*In what ways have you acted as a staff developer for your staff this year?

_____
_____
_____

Tip: *Every year, teachers and students come to the St. Joseph Academy Library to borrow scissors, markers, glue, and other production materials for class projects. This year, I decided to capitalize on that need. I purchased four heavy duty plastic bins and stocked them with class sets of scissors, rulers, a paper punch, markers, paper, a stapler, glue sticks, and other supplies. Then I bar coded the bins for easy circulation. I included the cost of the items in my budget, presented a rationale for the purchase, and the administration approved the purchase. The availability of the bins has promoted a lot of goodwill toward the library. In addition, when teachers stop in the library to check out the bins, I never miss an opportunity to talk with teachers about new print and electronic materials that may be useful to them in their teaching.*
    —Leanne Gilgenbach, St. Joseph Academy Library, Cleveland, Ohio (Library Talk March/April 2001)

February 3
1907   Walt Morey
1927   Joan Lowery Nixon

*In what ways can . . .

> "In a very real sense, people who have read good literature have lived more than people who cannot or will not read."
> —S. I. Hayakawa

_____
_____
_____
_____
_____

Tip: *Catch students' eyes and attention by using old CDs for library media center decorations. Collect and save advertising and out-of-date CDs. Use "sticky tack"/"gummy" to stick CDs directly on media center walls. Be sure to mount them shiny sides facing out. Rubber cement can be used to make CDs part of a bulletin board display. Use string to suspend CDs (back-to-back) from the library media center ceiling. Not only do the CDs get student's attention, they are also quick, bright, and attractive.*
    —Deb Logan, Taft Middle School, Marion, Ohio (Library Talk September/October 2000)

February 4 1925 Russell Hoban

> "Some books are to be tasted, others to be swallowed, and some few to be chewed and digested."
> —Francis Bacon "Of Studies." Essays II

Tip: The presentations of visiting authors are more enjoyable if students have read or heard the author's books. To make a few books go a long way, involve teachers in a drawing. Teachers enter each time they read one of the author's books to their classes. Just before the visit, draw several names. If you have funds, give away autographed books. If funds are tight, take photos of the winners with the author, or invite the winners to a lunch with your special guest.
—Pat Miller, Austin Parkway Elementary School, Sugar Land, Texas (Library Talk January/February 2002)

February 5 1924 Patricia Lauber

*When is your least productive time of the day? Why is it? What can you do to improve your productivity at that time?

> "Read in order to live."
> —Gustave Flaubert

Tip: I collected my student aides' e-mail addresses so I can send them notes of things I've forgotten to tell them, as well as reminders when they forget to bring in necessary paperwork.
—Anitra Gordon, Lincoln High School, Ypsilanti, MI (The Book Report March/April 2002)

February 6

*What are three ways you could make your day go smoother?

_____
_____
_____
_____
_____
_____
_____

> "Shera's Two Laws of Cataloguing.
> Law #1: No cataloger will accept the work of any other cataloger.
> Law #2: No cataloger will accept his/her own work six months after the cataloging."
> —Jesse Shera, University of Illinois, Graduate School of Library Science *Occasional Paper #131*

Tip: A good place to find out-of-print books at a reasonable cost is eBay. <www.ebay.com>

February 7

1812	Charles Dickens
1908	Fred Gipson
1867	Laura Ingalls Wilder

*Which word best describes your life—exciting, organized, dull, challenging? Why?

> "I am beginning to learn that it is the sweet, simple things of life which are the real ones after all."
> —Laura Ingalls Wilder

_____
_____
_____
_____
_____
_____

Tip: Every year choose two picture book authors and two fiction authors and make sure you have complete collections of all their works. In a few years, you will have several authors that teachers may choose from to do author studies.

February 8
1934 Anne Rockwell
1828 Jules Verne

*The best that can happen is . . .

_____
_____
_____
_____
_____

> *"The first thing naturally when one enters a scholar's study or library, is to look at his books. One gets the notion very speedily of his tastes and the range of his pursuits by a glance round his bookshelves."*
> —*Oliver Wendell Holmes,*
> The Poet at the Breakfast Table

Tip: Does your collection represent a diverse population? Pull a random sample of 20 books from each collection (i.e., biographies, fiction, non-fiction, easy). Examine each book. Is there a balance of female and male characters? Are different cultures represented? Is the content accurate? Do the books portray negative stereotypes? Is the terminology up to date?

February 9 1908 Hilda Van Stockum

*If only I had . . .

_____
_____
_____
_____
_____

Tip: I catalog and enter each issue of four different history magazines (Calliope, Faces, Cobblestone, and Footsteps) into our automated circulation system. We shelve them in the magazine room just like other periodicals. They are wonderful publications and come in handy when we need additional resources. Students can access them by title or subject. Schools may choose to circulate the periodicals or keep them as reference tools. We do not circulate them, and we have issues dating back to 1990.

—*Laura J. Viau, Monroe Middle School, Rochester, New York* (The Book Report *November/December 2001)*

February 10
1930 Elaine Konigsburg
1775 Charles Lamb

> "Libraries are as the shrines where all the relics of the ancient saints, full of true virtue, and that without delusion or imposture, are preserved and reposed."
> —Francis Bacon
> (1561–1626)

Tip: If you collect clip art, put it in folders labeled with the sources you use. In each folder, copy each source's stipulations for using their clip art and the URL for the site into a word processing document. In this way, you can use the clip art in the future, and won't have to wonder where it came from or if there were guidelines for using it. You might also create a database so that you can easily search for certain types of clip art in your source folders.
—Cathy Hart, Perry Middle School, Worthington, Ohio (**The Book Report** *March/April 2001*)

February 11
1939 Jane Yolen

Tip: When you have to make future follow up calls, place an appointment in your computer scheduler including the name of the person to call, the phone number, and what the call is about. That way, you will not have to try to remember to call them back—the computer will remind you to do so.

February 12 1938 Judy Blume
1960 Almira Astudillo Gilles

> *"I have always imagined that paradise will be a kind of library."*
> —*Jorge Luis Borges*
> *(1899–1986)*

Tip: Madrigal dinner theaters are becoming quite popular in many high schools, but finding costumes can be difficult. Save your drama director some costume research time by locating a copy of Aliki's picture book Medieval Feast (Crowell 1983). Aliki completed extensive research to create her illustrations; both the designs and colors are accurate.
—Sharron L. McElmeel, Cedar Rapids, Iowa (The Book Report *November/December 2000*)

February 13 1881 Eleanor Farjeon
1928 William Mayne
1945 William Sleator

> *"A truly great book should be read in youth, once again in maturity and once more in old age, as a fine building should be seen by morning light, at noon and by moonlight."*
> —*Robertson Davies*
> *(1913–1995)*

Tip: Books for Babies. When a student has a new brother or sister, donate an inexpensive paperback to the new baby along with a certificate of congratulations. Take a picture of the older sibling holding the certificate and the book and display these in the library. Parents really appreciate this gesture, and they are in turn very supportive of your program.

February 14   Valentines Day!
    1942   Jamake Highwater
    1952   George Shannon

> "For the civilized world accepts as unforgivable sin. Any talking out loud with any librarian."
> —Meredeth Wilson, "Marian the Librarian," from The Music Man

February 15
    1928   Norman Bridwell
    1929   Doris Orgel

> "Writing is the monumentally complex operation whereby experience, insight, and imagination are distilled into language; reading is the equally complex operation that disperses these distilled elements into another person's life."
> —Sven Birkerts, The Gutenberg Elegies

Tip: Place red and green plastic glasses upside down on top of your OPAC monitors. Tell students to keep the green glass on top of the red one unless they need help. Tell them that if they need assistance, they should place the red glass on top of the green one.

Journal Pages   *23*

February 16

> "The reflections and histories of men and women throughout the world are contained in books.... America's greatness is not only recorded in books, but it is also dependent upon each and every citizen being able to utilize public libraries."
> —Terence Cooke
> (1921–1983)

Tip: To get chewing gum out of carpet, fill a plastic sandwich bag with ice and seal. Place the bag over the gum and let it sit for 20 minutes. This should freeze the gum enough so that it can be scraped off with a scraper.

February 17

1879	Dorothy Canfield Fisher
1912	Andre Norton
1928	Robert Newton Peck
1948	Susan Beth Pfeffer
1912	Virginia Sorensen

> "A problem is a chance for you to do your best."
> —Duke Ellington

*How is your current check-out system working? Are there areas that could be streamlined?

Tip: Do not have a "To File" pile. Instead, file everything as you go along. You will not have more time "later." The "To File" pile just continues to grow.

February 18

> "Our high respect for a well read person is praise enough for literature."
> —Ralph Waldo Emerson
> (1803–1882)

Tip: Use a date stamp to date your lesson plans, notes, anything that you might look at later. It just takes a second and you will know at a glance when you received that note from a parent, wrote that plan, or first saw that great fundraising idea.

February 19
1903 Louis Slobodkin
1952 Amy Tan

*How are you helping your students become critical readers? What do you think are the critical attributes of a good reader? How can you move students to the next level of reading?

> "The world may be full of fourth-rate writers but it's also full of fourth-rate readers."
> —Stan Barsto

February 18

> "Our high respect for a well read person is praise enough for literature."
> —Ralph Waldo Emerson
> (1803–1882)

Tip: Use a date stamp to date your lesson plans, notes, anything that you might look at later. It just takes a second and you will know at a glance when you received that note from a parent, wrote that plan, or first saw that great fundraising idea.

February 19

1903 Louis Slobodkin
1952 Amy Tan

*How are you helping your students become critical readers? What do you think are the critical attributes of a good reader? How can you move students to the next level of reading?

> "The world may be full of fourth-rate writers but it's also full of fourth-rate readers."
> —Stan Barsto

February 20

Tip: To keep paperback books forward on the shelf, I buy the plastic corner strips that you can purchase at discount and hardware stores to keep wallpaper safe and secure on corners. I cut them to fit the shelves and use double stick tape to keep them in place.
   —*Lynette Mitchell, Library Media Specialist, Cistrus County Schools, Withlacoochee Technical Institute, Inverness, Florida* (The Book Report September/October 2002)

February 21

> "Reading maketh a full man; conference a ready man; and writing an exact man."
> —*Francis Bacon,* **The Essayes or Cousels, Civill and Morall**

Tip: I use solid-color plastic tablecloths to cover the backgrounds of the library showcase. They're bigger than any paper I could buy, cheap, and they don't tear.
   —*Diane Alexander, Liberty High School, Brentwood, California* (The Book Report May/June 2002)

February 22

> *"One should not read to swallow all, but rather see what one has use for."*
> —Henrik Ibsen
> (1828–1906)

Tip: After you have just received a big shipment of books you have ordered, send out an invitation for tea and cookies to the staff to preview the new holdings.

February 23

1932   C.S. Adler
1899   Eric Kastner

> *"How can you dare teach a man to read until you've taught him everything else first?"*
> —George Bernard Shaw
> (1856–1950)

Tip: If you serve it, they will come. Have a special little "school staff only" candy dish in the library and let the staff know about it. It will bring teachers into the library!

February 24   1786   Wilhelm Grimm

> *"Education is our passport to the future, for tomorrow belongs to the people who prepare for it today."*
> —*Malcolm X*

February 25
1862   Helen Brodie Bannerman
1914   Frank Bonham
1942   Cynthia Voigt

> *"Read the best books first, or you may not have a chance to read them at all."*
> —*Henry David Thoreau*
> *(1817–1862)*

February 26   1913   Miriam Young

___

Tip: Label copy paper boxes with each teacher's name and room number. Each morning, student helpers whose classes will come to the library that day use the boxes to return their classes books. Books can be quietly checked in, renewal books left in boxes, and overdue lists printed before classes arrive.
  —Pat Miller Walker, Station School, Sugar Land, Texas (Library Talk *September/ October 2001*)

February 27
1919   Florence Perry Heide
1807   Henry W. Longfellow
1850   Laura Richards
1935   Uri Shulevitz

*Why are you proud to be a media specialist?

> "Far and away the best prize that life has to offer is the chance to work hard at work worth doing."
> —Theodore Roosevelt

___

Tip: I solved my problem of crowd control in the library by tying the privilege of off-hours access into our Accelerated Reader program. Every nine weeks, I issue "High Point" passes to the top 30 AR readers in the school. This pass entitles them to free access to the library before and after school and during lunch. These passes are a major status symbol, and the kids who earn them are very proud of them. They use the computers, read, chat, play games, help me with tasks, and generally hang out. Age and reading level don't seem to matter—this last period I gave passes to eight first graders.
  —Gussje Moore, Librarian, Housman Elementary School, Spring Branch ISD, Houston, Texas (Library Talk *November/December 2000*)

February 28   1820   Sir John Tenniel

> *"Reading is a basic tool in the living of a good life."*
> —Mortimer J. Adler
> (1902–)

_____
_____
_____
_____
_____
_____
_____

Tip: Often backordered books come with fewer than five MARC records on the disk. After importing and indexing all the records, I move the write-protect tab on the disk from "read only" to "write" mode and use them instead of buying new disks for the library. It is convenient and a form of recycling.
—Sheryl Fullner, Nooksack Valley Middle School, Everson, WA (Library Talk January/February 2002)

March

The stormy March has come at last, / With wind, and cloud, and changing skies; / I hear the rushing of the blast / That through the snowy valley flies.
—William Cullen Bryant

March 1

_____
_____
_____
_____

Tip: In our media center we have a book security system that seemed out of place with our inviting reading atmosphere. We purchased a six-foot, tri-fold photo screen and inserted book cover jackets instead of photos in the picture windows. The result was a reading motivation display that hid our security system at the same time. We plan to change book covers as we purchase new books.
—Louise Scott and Kathey Davidson, Creekland Middle School, Lawrenceville, Georgia (The Book Report September/October 2000)

March 2
1933 Leo Dillon
1904 Dr. Seuss

*Are you where you thought you'd be ten years ago? Where will you be ten years from now? How do you plan to get there?

> "You have brains in your head. / You have feet in your shoes. / You can steer yourself any direction you choose. / You're on your own. And you know what you know. / And YOU are the one who'll decide where to go....OH! THE PLACES YOU'LL GO!"
> —Dr. Seuss

_____

_____

_____

_____

Tip: On March 2, we asked the school's cafeteria to serve green eggs and ham for breakfast that morning. We invited parents to attend and older students to stroll the breakfast area reciting some of their favorite verses from Dr. Seuss' books. As breakfast eaters went through the line, we gave them each a label printed in green text reading, "Happy Birthday, Dr. Seuss. I ate green eggs and ham today at _____ School." This birthday celebration day has become so popular we now have to sell advanced tickets to make sure we have enough food.
—Sharron L. McElmeel, Cedar Rapids, Iowa (Library Talk November/December 2000)

March 3
1938 Patricia MacLachlan

> "If the riches of the Indies, or the crowns of all the kingdoms of Europe, were laid at my feet in exchange for my love of reading, I would spurn them all."
> —Francois FéNelon

_____

32 Day by Day: Professional Journaling for Library Media Specialists

March 4   1906   Meindert DeJong

*What is something you do well? How can you share this with your supervisor?

> "The reflections and histories of men and women throughout the world are contained in books.... America's greatness is not only recorded in books, but it is also dependent upon each and every citizen being able to utilize public libraries."
> —Terence Cooke (1921–1983)

Tip: To help our middle school students to be responsible for their own library patron cards, we give each child a plastic, self-sealing snack bag and tape it to a common page in their agenda book during orientation. Because the agenda is used as their pass, students always carry their cards!
   —Carolyn Oakly, Henrico Count Public Schools, Richmond, Virginia (The Book Report *September/October 2001*)

March 5   1946   Mem Fox
             1941   Errol LeCain
             1853   Howard Pyle

> "Try not. Do or do not. There is no try."
> —*Yoda from* The Empire Strikes Back

Tip: To promote reading and researching using the 500's Dewey class, try a "Pet Show." Students can bring a stuffed animal for a research project. If you can, invite real animals to the library. The children will respond very well.
   —Madeleine Hoss, Metcalf Laboratory School, Illinois State University, Normal, Illinois (Library Talk *September/October 2001*)

March 6   1949   Thacher Hurd

*What questions do you have about your choice of careers? Would you make this same choice if you had it to do over again?

___
___
___

Tip: I post a question of the week outside the library door. Questions are diversified, so different reference materials must be used to answer each one. The questions may relate to the month, such as Black History Month, or to a holiday, such as St. Patrick's Day. Students participate by writing the answer to the question, their name, and their teacher's name on an answer slip and dropping it into a box. Every Monday, the box is emptied and the answers checked. One name is drawn from the correct responses. This person won a small prize. All the correct answers are saved until the end of the month when one name is drawn to win a free paperback book.
   —*Norma Uphold, Menallen Elementary School, Uniontown, Pennsylvania (Library Talk November/ December 2000)*

March 7

> "There is no true love without some sensuality. One is not happy in books unless one loves to caress them."
> —*Anatole France*, On Life and Letters, *1914*

March 8   1939   Trina Schart Hyman

*How do you feel you are doing with time management? What is your biggest time waster? What part of your time management system is really working for you?

> "From mine own library with volumes that I prize above my dukedom."
> —William Shakespeare, The Tempest *(Act I, sc. ii, L. 166)*

_____
_____
_____
_____

Tip: I had a problem with students walking out with certain magazines so I put barcode labels on file folders and keep them in a file cabinet at the desk. Students pick out the magazines they want, I check the folder out and keep it at the desk, then check it back in when the magazine is returned. This has cut down thefts 100%.
    —*Harolyn Legg, Liberty High School, Findlay, Ohio* (The Book Report *September/October 2000*)

March 9   1859   Kenneth Grahame
              1908   Joseph Krumgold

> "A library is not a luxury but one of the necessities of life."
> —Henry Ward Beecher

_____
_____
_____
_____
_____
_____

Tip: When our K-5 school held a Math Night for Parents, they were asked to sign up in each classroom they visited. At regular intervals, the sign-up slips were taken to the office where a drawing was held. The prize—a book connected to mathematics that they could share with their children. Popular choices were The Doorbell Rang by Pat Hutchins, How to make a Million by David M. Scwartz, and any one of the Math-Start titles by Stuart Murphy.
    —*Sharron L. McElmeel, Cedar Rapids, Iowa* (Library Talk *September/October 2000*)

March 10   1920   Jack Kent

> "Surviving and thriving as a professional today demands two new approaches to the written word. First, it requires a new approach to orchestrating information, by skillfully choosing what to read and what to ignore. Second, it requires a new approach to integrating information, by reading faster and with greater comprehension."
> —Jimmy Calano

Tip: Subscribe to professional journals such as LMC (Library Media Connection). The book reviews alone are worth the subscription costs, and the articles keep you current in your field.

March 11   1893   Wanda Gag
   1916   Ezra Jack Keats

*What is something that really makes you angry? How can you express your anger in a healthier manner?

> "A book is solitude, privacy; it is a way of holding the self apart from the crush of the outer world."
> —Sven Birkerts, The Gutenberg Elegies

Tip: Do a library lesson with students on which books would make a great gift. Have students write their suggestions for good gift books on slips of paper with a present clip art on it. Make a display of all of their suggestions on one large gift box. Maybe the next time they are invited to a birthday party, they will think of bringing a book or asking for books when it is their turn for a present!

March 12   1936   Virginia Hamilton

> "Libraries are as the shrines where all the relics of the ancient saints, full of true virtue, and that without delusion or imposture, are preserved and reposed."
> —Francis Bacon (1561–1626)

March 13   1933   Diane Dillon
1928   Ellen Raskin
1933   Thomas Rockwell

*Is your current technology adequate to meet the needs of your school? What would you like to learn more about video editing, digital camera, and web page design? How could new skills enhance your program?

> "To me, the computer is just another tool. It's like a pen. You have to have a pen, and know penmanship, but neither will write the book for you."
> —Red Burns, Interactive Telecommunications Program chairperson, New York University's Tisch School of Arts

Tip: It is worth your time to take a basic computer/printer repair class. It will save you the aggravation of waiting for a repair person, and you will be able to fix minor glitches on your own.

March 14   1889   Marguerite DeAngeli

> "My experience with public libraries is that the first volume of the book I inquire for is out, unless I happen to want the second, when that is out."
> —Oliver Wendell Holmes, The Poet at the Breakfast Table

Tip: A fun fundraiser for the library is to ask for donations of books students are no longer using. Place the books on long tables, and hold a sale with prices at 25 or 50 cents each. Donate leftover books to a local food bank or another charity that could use the books. You can also use the sales proceeds to donate to a local charity or to purchase something special for the school. This is a good end-of-the-year activity so students will have plenty to read over vacation.

March 15

Tip: The most useful materials in the world will remain on the shelf, unused, if the library's catalog database is not user-friendly. A database is only as good as its material tracings and summaries, but because companies are cutting cataloging costs, at least two-thirds of the materials I order arrive without summaries, tracing, or both. I create my own summaries and tracings for the library's catalog using chapter titles and indexes for nonfiction books and book related sites on the Internet for fiction and sometimes nonfiction books. I also keep book reviews as I prepare my order, file these reviews alphabetically by author after the books arrive, and refer to them when writing summaries.
    *—Jeanette Roberts, Moundridge (Kansas) High School (*The Book Report *September/October 2000)*

March 16 1920 Sid Fleishman

March 17 St. Patrick's Day

    1846   Kate Greenaway
    1933   Penelope Lively
    1934   Zibby Oneal

* I really need to . . .

> "A conventional good read is usually a bad read, a relaxing bath in what we know already. A true good read is surely an act of innovative creation in which we, the readers, become conspirators."
> —Malcolm Bradbury (1932–)

    On St. Patrick's Day, make cut outs of several Leprechaun feet. Place them on the floor as if they are walking to a table. With the cutouts on the floor, sprinkle baking soda all around the footprints. Lift the cut outs up and you will have a trail of footprints leading to the table. Place a pot (buy a clearance black cauldron after Halloween) on the table and fill it with great books to be checked out. Books are the best kind of treasure! Plus, the baking soda will make the carpet smell good after it is vacuumed up!

March 18

*I am very pleased about . . .

_____

_____

_____

_____

> "Doing research on the Web is like using a library assembled piecemeal by pack rats and vandalized nightly."
> —Roger Ebert, Yahoo! Internet Life *column*, September 1998, p. 66

Tip: Showcasing new materials is a priority to get students, faculty, and administrators to check them out. Each month, select at least three teachers to sample new library resources (a combination of books, videos, and CDs) and give you written or oral feedback on these items. Then make a display with the teachers' school pictures along with their reviews. Students and other teachers love to see what teachers are reading and can't wait to check out the new items.
   —*Mercedes Smith, Bishop Kenny High School, Jacksonville, Florida* (The Book Report *September/October 2001*)

March 19   1848   James Otis

*What have you been putting off doing? Why haven't you done it? What would help you to get it done?

_____

_____

_____

_____

_____

Tip: On open house night, for parents, the librarian offers free plastic bags with local bookstore advertising to hold all the teacher handouts. The bags make it more likely that the handouts will make it home. Besides, parents love getting something for free.
   —*Peggy Fleming, Churchville-Chili Senior High School, Churchville, New York* (The Book Report *November/December 2000*)

March 20
1926	Mitsumasa Anno
1937	Lois Lowry
1942	Ellen Conford

*What books have become a part of you? How has a book shaped the person you are today?

> "I am a part of everything that I have read."
> —John Kieran

_____

_____

_____

_____

Tip: To make sure that my parent volunteers always know what to do and how to do it, I laminated instructions and taped them to the top of the circulation desk. One sheet lists all the duties of the parent volunteers. The other sheet has step-by-step instructions for checking books in, out, and renewing them. I made them in Print Shop so they look nice. The checkout instructions are handy for the student assistants too.
    —*Yapha Nussbaum Mason, Brentwood School Librarian, Los Angeles (*The Book Report *January/February 2001)*

March 21
1905	Phyllis McGinley

*It is easy to get caught up in the negative attitudes of coworkers. What have you had to do to avoid this? How can you contribute to a positive work atmosphere?

> "It takes but one positive thought when given a chance to survive and thrive to overpower an entire army of negative thoughts."
> —Robert Schuller

_____

_____

_____

_____

Tip: The second you're finished using something, put it away immediately. The sooner the item is back in its designated home, the less likely it will end up lost. Plus, at a later date, you'll be able to find it when you need it.

Journal Pages *41*

March 22   1846   Randolph Caldecott

*What book do you think should have won the Caldecott or the Newbery? Why do you think this book was overlooked? If you were on the committee, what qualities would you be looking for in an award-winning book?

_____
_____
_____
_____

Tip: *Invite a different academic department into the library each month to go through the section(s) of the collection that apply to the curriculum. Encourage staff members to weed out and to suggest new titles for purchase. Offer food as an incentive. This works well on an every two or three year basis. It also gets people into the library who might not get there any other way.*
—Julie Burwinkel, Ursuline Academy, Cincinnatti, Ohio (The Book Report *September/October 2000*)

March 23   1912   Eleanor Cameron

*How does your vision of how a school should look and be run compare with your current situation?

_____
_____
_____
_____
_____

> "That I can read and be happy while I am reading, is a great blessing. Could I have remembered, as some men do, what I read, I should have been able to call myself an educated man. But that power I have never possessed. Something is always left—something dim and inaccurate—but still something sufficient to preserve the taste for more. I am inclined to think that it is so with most readers."
> —Anthony Trollope
> (1815–1882)

Tip: *Keep a two pocket folder for each teacher. Tests or makeup work to be done in the library go in the left-hand pocket with the students' names on them. Completed work goes in the right-hand pocket. Place the folders in a simple open file, such as "in" box. Teachers come in daily to check their folders for completed work and to add new items.*
—Anne Shipley, Waterloo, New York (The Book Report *September/October 2000*)

March 24   1920   Bill Cleaver

*Would someone brand new to the building know where to find things in your library without asking? Does the layout make sense? Are things placed where they could be found easily? What needs to be changed?

> *"Any book which is at all important should be reread immediately."*
> —Arthur Schopenhauer

_____
_____
_____
_____
_____
_____
_____

Tip: Take a day and go visit other library programs in your area. It can be very eye opening to see how other libraries are set up and run. Be sure to take your journal or another writing pad to note the good ideas you want to remember!

March 25

*I really want to read the following books:

> *"Leer is poder." (Reading is power.)*
> —Spanish version of ALA's graphics posters.

_____
_____
_____
_____
_____
_____
_____
_____

Tip: Area rugs are inexpensive at discount stores. These rugs can be used to help bring in a little color to the library.

March 26
1874 Robert Frost
1908 Betty MacDonald
1953 Jerry Pallota

*I am so frustrated about . . .

> "About all we can really say in paper's favor is that it's lighter than clay, less awkward than papyrus, and cheaper than parchment."
> —*Gregory J.E. Rawlins,*
> **Moths to the Flame**

Tip: Volunteer to help at your state library conference. Conference planning takes many hours and is mainly done by volunteers. Even if you just work at the hospitality booth for an hour, it is a big help to the conference team. This is also a good way to meet people who are involved in your field.

March 27

*Wisdom and intelligence are different concepts. Who do you know that is wise? What makes them wise?

> "Books give not wisdom where none was before. But where some is, there reading makes it more."
> —*John Harington*

Tip: Put things you need for work in your car the night before. It is easy to overlook that book bag on the counter in the morning rush.

March 28
1924   Byrd Baylor
1920   Mary Stolz

*The best thing that happened today was . . .

> *"Imagination is more important than knowledge. Knowledge is limited. Imagination encircles the world."*
> —Albert Einstein

___

Tip: Assemble a small first-aid kit for the library with Band-Aids, antiseptic wipes, gauze pads, and other items that might come in handy.

March 29

*In order to improve communication with administration, I plan to . . .

> *"Once we have learned to read, meanings of words can somehow register without consciousness."*
> —Anthony Marcel

___

Tip: Keep all your guarantees/warranties together in one place, and keep them until they have expired.

Journal Pages 45

March 30   1820   Anna Sewell

*Who or what has had a strong influence in your life?

> "Don't ask me who's influenced me. A lion is made up of the lambs he's digested, and I've been reading all my life."
> —Giorgos Seferis

_____
_____
_____
_____
_____
_____
_____

Tip: Displaying a new or attractively covered book at the circulation desk with a large "ASK ME" bookmark protruding from its pages is a good way to talk it up to students. Just make sure the staff know why it would make a good read or whose class project it supports. And be sure to have several of these under the counter; they may not stay long!
—Mary Strazdas, Student, San Jose State University, SLIS (Library Talk January/February 2002)

March 31   1844   Andrew Lang

*What is your favorite way to unwind? What recharges your soul?

> "Education is what survives when what has been learned has been forgotten."
> —B.F. Skinner

_____
_____
_____
_____
_____
_____
_____
_____

Tip: Schedule 15 minutes at the end of the day just to go around and pick things up and straighten up. It will be so much nicer the next morning not to have to start the day with a mess.

April

National Library Week is in April

"April cold with dropping rain
and lilacs brings again,
The whistle of returning birds
And trumpet-lowing of the herds."
—*Ralph Waldo Emerson*

April 1   April Fool's Day
   1926   Anne McCaffrey
   1933   Jan Wahl

*Are you having fun? What parts of your job do you really look forward to doing? How can you make the other parts more fun?

_____

_____

_____

Tip: When redesigning a library, be sure to angle all shelving so that you can see between the rows from the charge desk.
   —*Ann Patterson, Lindsay Middle School, Hampton, Virginia* (Library Talk *January/February 2002*)

April 2   1805   Hans Christian Anderson
   1783   Washington Irving

"In the case of good books, the point is not to see how many of them you can get through, but rather how many can get through to you."
   —*Mortimer J. Adler*

_____

_____

_____

_____

_____

Tip: Need to spread the word to get your co-workers attention? Post staff messages over the school's photocopier machines, on the wall behind shared phones, in the bathroom, and by teacher's mailboxes. If you have a flexible schedule, these locations are also effective places to post a copy.
   —*Deb Logan, Taft Middle School, Marion, Ohio* (Library Talk *May/June 2001*)

April 3

> "Whenever a man does a thoroughly stupid thing, it is always from the noblest motives."
> —Oscar Wilde, **The Picture of Dorian Gray**

Tip: You have an opportunity to get one or two books autographed. What do you do? Do you have the school's copies autographed, knowing that they might be lost or chewed up the first time they are checked out? Do you get your personal copies autographed, knowing that they will be treasured—but feeling bad that your students will not have access to them? Compromise by having your personal copies autographed to you and your students: To Mrs. Logan and her library friends . . . Share the autograph, how you got it, and stories about the author with your students for many years to come.
—Deb Logan, Taft Middle School, Marion, Ohio (Library Talk March/April 2001)

April 4
1942 Elizabeth Levy
1906 Glen Rounds

*I need to convince my principal that . . .

> "My lifelong love affair with books and reading continues unaffected by automation, computers, and all other forms of twentieth-century gadgetry."
> —Robert Downs, **Books in My Life**

Tip: Have "Muffins with Mom" and "Doughnuts with Dad" days in the library.

April 5   1834   Frank Stockton

*What five things are most important in your life right now? Are those five things getting the most of your time?

> "Literature is news that stays news."
> —Ezra Pound

_____
_____
_____
_____
_____
_____
_____

*Tip: Rename your "Easy" section to the "Everybody" section. That way everyone will feel comfortable checking out picture books. Then do a lesson with your older students on how some pictures are really for older readers. (*Math Curse* for example).*

April 6

*If only . . . . . . then . . . . .

> "A university is just a group of buildings gathered around a library."
> —Shelby Foote

_____
_____
_____
_____

Tip: No time for staff development? MOLE (Mentoring OnLine for Excellence) can provide teachers with an effective tool for utilizing and investigating Web resources that enhance student learning. Initiate a brief e-mail to all teachers. In the e-mail, include one or two URLs for teachers to click on and investigate. Teachers, at a time convenient for them, are then exposed to a variety of sites and resources. Teachers can send a site suggestion back to the MOLE coordinator, who then features it in the MOLE system. Desktop staff development promotes educational objectives and is a great motivator for teachers, as technology becomes a tool for discovery.
—Terry Zabloki, Boerne (Texas) High School (**The Book Report** *November/December 2001*)

April 7   1929   Donald Carrick

> *"Employ your time in improving yourself by other men's writing so that you shall come easily by what others have labored hard for."*
> —*Socrates (469–399 BC)*

Tip: To promote books and technology, use your digital camera to take pictures of students reading a book, newspaper, or magazine during National Library Week in April. After cropping and labeling each picture with "National Library Week and the date, insert them into mouse pads located by the computers in the library media center. Students love to see themselves in pictures!
—*Mary N. Stallings, Poquoson (Virginia) High School (Library Talk March/April 2002)*
(You could also load the pictures on your library computers and have them randomly come up for your screen saver—Karen Larsen)

April 8

*What is the best advice you ever received?

Tip: When I receive an e-mail from one of the many sites on which my e-mail address is linked, knowing where the person found my address is sometimes difficult. I solved this problem by changing the way I link my e-mail address. Instead of a link created in the usual manner as <A HREF= "mailto:mcelmeel@mcelmeel.com">, which would indeed bring up a template for a mail message, I now include a fake name that indicates how the e-mail link has been accessed. For example: on a page sharing brown bag lunch ideas for a reading institute, the hyperlink was coded as <A HREF= "mailto:Brown Bag<mcelmeel@mcelmeel.com">. On another page where a colleagues were contacting me because my affiliation with a local reading council, the hyperlink read <A HREF= "mailto:Pres.CR Reading <mcelmeel@mcelmeel.com>">. The pattern for coding this links is <A HREF= "mailto:fake-name<yourusername@youruserdomainname.com>">
—*Sharron L. McElmeel, Cedar Rapids, Iowa (Library Talk September/October 2001)*

April 9   1915   Leonard Wibberly

*What do you think staff members say to each other about your program when you're not around?

> *"There are perhaps no days of our childhood we lived so fully as those we believe we left without having lived them: those we spent with a favourite book."*
> —*Marcel Proust*

April 10   1897   Eric Knight
1903   Clare Newberry

*Who was your favorite teacher and why? What made this person such a good teacher?

> *"A little library growing each year is an honorable part of a man's history."*
> —*Henry Ward Beecher*

April 11

*What would you invent to make life better in the library?

> "The most technologically efficient machine that man has ever invented is the book."
> —*Northrop Frye*

April 12

    1916   Beverly Cleary
    1911   Barbara Corcoran
    1907   Hardie Gramatky

> "The librarian's mission should be, not like up to now, a mere handling of the book as an object, but rather a know how (mise au point) of the book as a vital function."
> —*Jose Ortega y Gasset,*
> **Mission del Bibliotecario**

Tip: On e-mail, don't use the "Reply all" function unless you absolutely have to reply to everyone as this creates unnecessary e-mails to be read by other people.

April 13
1893   Genevieve Foster
1902   Marguerite Henry

*If someone were to ask me if I thought this was a good profession to enter, I would tell him or her . . .

> "The delights of reading impart the vivacity of youth even to old age."
> —Isaac D'Israeli (1766–1848)

_____
_____
_____
_____
_____
_____

    Tip: Give out the "Library" award at the end of the year to the graduating student you think would make a good media specialist. Have a plaque made for the student and have a permanent plaque in the school that lists all of the previous winners.

April 14

*When is the busiest time of day in your library? How do you feel then?

> "No place affords a more striking conviction of the vanity of human hopes than a public library."
> —Samuel Johnson, **The Rambler**

_____
_____
_____
_____

    Tip: To make the library more accessible and comfortable to teenagers, I looked to local bookstores for decorating ideas. I bought some secondhand easy chairs, each under $30, from Goodwill and antique malls. Getting into the spirit of it, our principal made an announcement that teachers and parents who were redecorating could donate their old furniture to the library. That gained us four more wingback chairs. Students and teachers love the comfortable seating, and we've reached students who never before hung out in the library.
    —Laura Younkin, Ballard High School, Louisville, Kentucky (**The Book Report** January/February 2001)

April 15 Tax Day

*How did you budget and spend your money last year? How will you plan to use your money more effectively this year?

_____

_____

_____

_____

April 16
- 1922 John Christopher
- 1890 Gertrude Chandler Warner
- 1912 Garth Williams

*Where is your favorite place to read? What do you like to read when you just want to relax? Have you taken time for yourself lately to savor a good book?

> "The time to read is any time: no apparatus, no appointment of time and place, is necessary. It is the only art which can be practiced at any hour of the day or night, whenever the time and inclination comes, that is your time for reading; in joy or sorrow, health or illness."
> —Holbrook Jackson (1874–1948)

_____

_____

_____

_____

Tip: We have found that one way to build goodwill with your staff members is through their stomachs! We usually provide treats for the whole staff in the library a couple of times a year. One time is usually in observance of School Library Month in April. For example, insert bananas that have written on them "This banana is due in the library Friday between 11 am and 1 pm" into staff mailboxes. Then make banana splits when staff members bring in their bananas. We also put large plastic cups in mailboxes and attached a note inviting staff members to bring the cup in at a certain time. We then serve Italian sodas (this was a big hit!). This year we used paper "boats" and inserted a sail shaped note that invited staff to "Sail into the Library for a Treat!" We served strawberry shortcake with angel food cake.
    —Rosemary Knapp, Camas (Washington) High School (The Book Report *September/October 2000*)

April 17

> "Reading is not a duty, and has consequently no business to be made disagreeable."
> —Augustine Birrell (1850–1933)

April 18

*What worked really well in your last unit? What can you carry over to the next unit that you teach?

> "The size of the library media program, as indicated by the size of its staff and collection, is the best school predictor of academic achievement. Library media center expenditures predict the size the lmc's staff and collection and, in turn, academic achievement. The instructional role of the lmc shapes the collection and, in turn, academic achievement."
> —Keith Curry Lance "The Impact of School Library Media Centers on Academic Achievement: Colorado Study," *School Library Media Quarterly*

Tip: Make a time to get together with other librarians in your district. This can be an isolated position as you're the only one in the school doing it. It is important to share ideas and experiences with others in the same field.

April 19 1902 Jean Lee Latham

*What is something that really bugs you?

> "I have never known any distress that an hour's reading did not relieve."
> —Montesquieu

Tip: Get a large gallon glass jar from the cafeteria. Fill it with different small objects each month and have staff members and kids enter a contest to guess how many items are in the jar. This brings a lot of people into the library. Have a prize for the adult who comes closest and another for the student who comes the closest.

April 20 1826 Dinah Craik

*What knowledge do you wish you had learned before you started this job? What should be included in library classes to better prepare future librarians?

> "A man ought to read just as inclination leads him, for what he reads as a task will do him little good."
> —Samuel Johnson

Tip: I made attractive laminated signs that read, "computer in use." Students prop these up against the monitor (Usually using the keyboard to hold it in place) when they leave the computer to look for a book, indicating that their computer isn't available even if it appears to be. This way, they can continue working at the computer when they return. This is especially helpful with the second graders who are just learning to search the OPAC and find materials on their own in the library.
—Laura Mench, Lower School, Lake Ridge, Academy, North Ridgeville, Ohio (Library Talk November/December 2000)

April 21   1947   Barbara Park

*Whom do you appreciate? Why do you appreciate this person? How have you communicated your appreciation to this person?

> "Appreciation can make a day—even change a life. Your willingness to put it into words is all that is necessary."
> —Margaret Cousins

_____

_____

_____

_____

_____

_____

_____

Tip: Have thank you notes made up with your library logo on them. Each week send a note to someone who you appreciate and thank him or her for what they do.

April 22   Earth Day
       1943   Eileen Christelow
       1887   Kurt Wiese

> "Readers are plentiful: thinkers are rare."
> —Harriet Martineau

*Are you someone who loves to read or do you only read for work, not pleasure? Who influenced you in this direction? What factors facilitate people into becoming passionate readers? How can you help nurture this passion in the students with whom you work?

_____

_____

_____

_____

_____

_____

_____

April 23 1564 William Shakespeare

> "Reading is to the mind what exercise is to the body. It is wholesome and bracing for the mind to have its faculties kept on the stretch."
> —*Augustus Hare (1792–1834)*

April 24 1911 Evaline Ness
　　　　　　1914 Lynn Hall

> "A good education is not so much one which prepares a man to succeed in the world, as one which enables him to withstand a failure."
> —*Bernard Iddings Bell, chaplain, University of Chicago*

Tip: Purchase a small metal scraper. It is handy to use when cleaning tables and removing labels.

April 25 1873 Walter De La Mare
1892 Maud Hart Lovelace

> *"As a general rule, librarians are a kick in the pants socially, often full of good humor, progressive, and, naturally, well read."*
> —Bill Hall, cited in **American Libraries**

April 26 1935 Patricia Reilly Giff
1938 Lee Bennett Hopkins

> *"A bookstore is one of the only pieces of evidence we have that people are still thinking."*
> —Jerry Seinfeld

April 27 1898 Ludwig Bemelmans
              1936 John Burningham

*What is holding you back from accomplishing what you want to accomplish? How can you address these concerns?

_____
_____
_____
_____
_____
_____

> "So two decades from now paper books may be the phonograph records of their time. They'll exist for historical, sentimental, or ceremonial reasons. And for the wealthy, they'll still make perfectly good furniture. But eventually they'll go the way of the vacuum tube, which, legend tells us, existed in the 1940s and 1950s."
> —Gregory J.E. Rawlins, Moths to the Flame

Tip: Turn off the automatic e-mail notification on your computer. Check your e-mail when it is convenient for you instead of having it interrupt your train of thought.

April 28 Great Poetry Reading Day
            1934 Lois Duncan
            1935 Ben Shecter

*Who is someone that has influenced your career selection? How did this person help you get where you are today?

> "*Dynasty* was the opportunity to take charge of my career rather than waiting around like a library book waiting to be loaned out."
> —Joan Collins (1933–)

_____
_____
_____
_____
_____
_____

Tip: Take a look at your career books. Are they current? Do they portray both men and women? Are different cultures represented? To make a display of career books, gather job applications from local businesses as well as job descriptions off the Internet. Intersperse these with the career books on a table or a display cabinet.

April 29   1953   Nicole Rubel
              1937   Jill Paton Walsh

> *"The book to read is not the one which thinks for you, but the one which makes you think."*
> —*James McCosh*

Tip: Take the time to train your media center staff, volunteers, or student helpers to do tasks that you currently do, but someone else could do with a little training. Even though you think it is easier to do a task that you can do yourself in 10 minutes, by delegating this task to another, you can save yourself hours or days over a school year.

April 30   1936   Harriet Sobol

*What has been the most fun activity at school so far? Why is it important to bring "fun" activities into a school?

> *"Libraries is fun! They gots lots of tables to crawl under."*
> —(Rugrats *episode. Line spoken by the character of Lil DeVille)*

 May

"Yesterday, being the first of May, a number of persons went into the fields and bathed their faces with the dew on the grass, with the idea that it would render them beautiful."
—*London paper, 1791*

May is National Physical Fitness & Sports Month — Create a display of sports books

Mother's Day is in May.

May 1 *It's May Day! Surprise someone with a basket of flowers.*

> *"A good education is the next best thing to a pushy mother."*
> —*Charles Shultz*, Peanuts

Tip: My library is in a portable building at the farthest corner of the school campus. We purchased Radio Flyer wagons for students to use when returning books for a class. Everyone loves them. We use the wooden side panels to advertise upcoming events.
—*Babette Longobardi, Helen Estock Elementary, Tustin, California* (Library Talk *May/June 2001*)

May 2 *Thank Your School Librarian Day*

May 3   1947   Mavis Jukes

> "Until I feared I would lose it, I never loved to read. One does not love breathing."
> —Harper Lee

Tip: Don't spend money on prizes when you play games. Instead, allow the winners to check out one extra book that week. It's motivational, free, and increases book circulation.
—Pat Miller, Walker Station Elementary, Sugar Land, Texas (Library Talk *March/April 2001*)

May 4   1932   Beverly Butler

> "Two forces are successfully influencing the education of a cultivated man: art and science. Both are united in the book."
> —Maksim Gorky
> (1868–1936)

Tip: You should take a hard look at your science books (the 500's) at least every five years. This information is constantly being updated. Check the copyright date of each book. Anything older than five years should be closely examined for accuracy. Anything older than 10 years should receive serious consideration for weeding.

May 5   Celebrate Cinco de Mayo!
1907   (Georges Remi) Herge

> *"Great writers are people like Emily Bronte who write out of limited experience and unlimited imagination."*
> —James Michener

Tip: Update your library Web page each month and check your links to make sure they are still working. Choose a date that is easy for you to remember, like payday, and update it then.

May 6
1931   Judy Delton
1914   Randall Jarrell
1910   Leo Lionni
1942   Giulio Maestro

Tip: If you are frequently called into the classroom to troubleshoot TV/VCR problems, try posting a troubleshooting guide on the VCR. We list the basics, such as "Check to make sure channel is set to 3" and "Check to make sure that the back of the VCR cable is connected to 'video out' on the VCR and to 'video in' on the back of the TV." The guide is laminated and then taped to the top of the VCR where is readily visible.
    —Jane Perry, Winslow Jr. High Library, St. Winslow, Maine (Library Talk September/ October 2001)

May 7 1932 Nonny Hogrogian

> "... I dream away my life in others' speculations. I love to lose myself in other mens minds. When I am not walking, I am reading; I cannot sit and think. Books think for me."
> —Charles Lamb (1775–1834)

Tip: Clean each piece of AV equipment as you check it back in at the end of the school year. Cover overhead projectors with large garbage bags to keep them clean over the summer.

May 8 1938 Milton Meltzer

> "Libraries are the wardrobes of literature, whence men, properly informed may bring forth something for ornament, much for curiosity, and more for use."
> —William Dyer (1636–1696)

May 9

1920 Richard Adams
1860 Sir James M. Barrie
1916 William Pene DuBois
1906 Eleanor Estes
1914 Keith Robertson

*If you were to write a children's book, what would your book be about?

> "The greatest gift is the passion for reading. It is cheap, it consoles, it distracts, it excites, it gives you knowledge of the world and experience of a wide kind. It is a moral illumination."
> —Elizabeth Hardwick (1916–)

Tip: In our library computer lab, we name each computer after a character [sic] in the zodiac. Each computer monitor bears a big label with its name (ie. Sagittarius, Libra, Leo) and is identified on the network by that name. Students who want to use these computers check out a plastic pass, a paddle matching a given computer. The paddle has a name label and barcode for easy checkout by our circulation system. Students love to ask for computers by name, and librarians can see at a glance that students are using the right computer.
—Paul Scaer, J.R. Masterman Lab and Demonstration School, Philadelphia, Pennsylvania
Library Talk *January/February 2002)*

May 10
1922 John Rowe Townsend

> "So many books, so little time."
> —T-shirt slogan

Tip: Have your students write book reviews. Then post these on your school's Web site.

May 11 1918 Sheila Burnford

> *"No entertainment is so cheap as reading, nor any pleasure so lasting."*
> —*Lady Mary Wortley Montagu (1689–1762)*

Tip: At the end of the year, order any projector bulbs you might need for the next school year so they are on hand the first day back.

May 12 1812 Edward Lear
            1921 Farley Mowat

> *"Librarians are almost always very helpful and often almost absurdly knowledgeable. Their skills are probably very underestimated and largely underemployed."*
> —*Charles Medwar,* **The Social Audit Consumer Handbook**

May 13 1938 Norma Klein
1938 Francine Pascal

> "When I want a book, it is as a tiger wants a sheep. I must have it with one spring, and, if I miss it, go away defeated and hungry."
> —Oliver Wendell Holmes, Sr., The Poet at the Breakfast Table

May 14 1929 George Selden

> "A great public library, in its catalogue and its physical disposition of its books on shelves, is the monument of literary genres."
> —Robert Melancon, World Literature Today

Tip: Sometimes MARC records are not available for ancient books, used books, or too new books. When I want to get a book on the shelf in a hurry, I do a quick, very abbreviated catalog record with just title, author, call number, and publishing info. I don't want to leave the record like that permanently, so I do these fast entries ALL IN CAPS, which not only allows me to type faster but also leaves a visual trail that I can pick up quickly when I scroll through that section of our collection. It also alerts me to the absence of added entries . . . if that's what I'm looking for. I also type NFC in a field I don't use so that I can do a global search for a batch of these Not Fully Catalogued items to update them when time permits. I type DLF for Don't Look Further on items that will probably never have records, such as some vanity-published books or old classics for which finding the correct edition out of hundreds would require hours of searching.

—Sheryl Kindle Fullner, Nooksack Valley Middle School, Everson, Washington (The Book Report *January/February 2002*)

May 15 1856 L. Frank Baum
1906 Ellen MacGregor
1931 Norma Fox Mazer
1891 Florence Crannell Means
1936 Paul Zindel

> "No matter how busy you may think you are, you must find time for reading, or surrender yourself to self-chosen ignorance."
> —Atwood H. Townsend

Tip: When someone asks you to do something that you are not sure you want to do, whether it is to serve on a committee or change a library policy, don't give an answer right away. Say, "Let me think about it for a while and I'll get back to you." It is important to give yourself time to make thoughtful decisions.

May 16 1950 Bruce Coville
1928 Betty Miles

> "Creativity is allowing yourself to make mistakes. Art is knowing which ones to keep."
> —Scott Adams

Tip: Weed out outdated and broken AV materials at the end of the year. Start a list and order replacement pieces you are going to need at the beginning of the year.

May 17   1939   Gary Paulsen

> *"It is the supreme art of the teacher to awaken joy in creative expression and knowledge."*
> —Albert Einstein

Tip: If at all possible, get away from the library for at least 20 minutes a day. It gives you a fresh perspective to get away from it all for a few minutes. A quick walk around the outside of the school is great for recharging your batteries.

May 18   1907   Irene Hunt
1925   Lillian Hoban

*How have you made a difference in a student's life this year?

> *"There are two ways of being creative. One can sing and dance. Or one can create an environment in which singers and dancers flourish."*
> —Warren Bennis

Tip: Since we all know you can never have enough PR (or time between classes!), I let my sixth grade classes do poster projects to create PR for the titles of our state student book award nominees. Each group of 3-4 took one book, read reviews of it, and designed posters to advertise that title. We then displayed them around the school. A side benefit was increased circulation with our poster designers!
—Mary Elizabet Butcher, Mt. Vernon (Indiana) Junior High School (Library Talk September/October 2000)

May 19 1921 Pauline Clarke
1936 Peter J. Lippman

> *"For one who reads, there is no limit to the number of lives that may be lived, for fiction, biography and history offer an inexhaustible number of lives in many parts of the world, in all periods of time."*
> —Louis L'amour
> (1908–1988)

May 20 1935 Carol Carrick

*If you had a $5,000 donation given to your library, how would you spend it?

> *"Choose an author as you choose a friend."*
> —Sir Christopher Wren
> (1632–1723)

Tip: Create a summer reading list for each grade level. Have students set their own goals for summer reading (i.e., number of pages, number of books, number of minutes per day). Have them create their own method of keeping track of their reading and turn it in the beginning of the next school year for a prize. For an example of this, visit:
<http://www.ad12.k12.co.us/cottoncreek/home.html>

May 21

*What is the most creative thing you have done while in this job?

> "There is creative reading as well as creative writing."
> —Ralph Waldo Emerson
> (1803–1882)

Tip: Be aware of how much of your day you spend socializing with others. While you may feel you need to create bonds with others, make sure it doesn't take up too much of your day.

May 22
1859 Arthur Conan Doyle
1933 Arnold Lobel

*What is the nicest thing any one ever said about you? What's the nicest thing you've ever said about someone else?

> "Master books, but do not let them master you. Read to live, not live to read."
> —Edward Bulwer-Lytton

May 23

1903   Scott O'Dell
1910   Margaret Wise Brown
1915   Oliver Butterworth
1935   Susan Cooper
1936   Peter Parnall

*How do you see this library five years from now? What changes will you have made?

> *"The great thing in this world is not so much where we are, but in what direction we are moving."*
> —Oliver Wendell Holmes

Tip: Send your graduating students to middle school with a mission to read! Near the end of the school year, carefully select books from your area middle school's library media center. Choose an intriguing collection of fiction and nonfiction books. Include some old favorites that can be found in both libraries. Select some appealing books that are "too old" for your elementary collection. Schedule times to book talk the books. You'll leave the students anxious to visit their new library media center.
—Deb Logan, Taft Middle School, Marion, Ohio (Library Talk *May/June 2001*)

May 24

Tip: I purchased a shelving unit that has nine bright-blue plastic tubs, which we use to assemble an assortment of books, at a teacher's request on a particular subject. I label the tubs with bright signs so students can locate them easily. Our student librarians also compiled their favorite reads in one tub.
—Ellen Goldfinch, Bishop's College School, Lennoxville, Quebec (Library Talk *March/April 2002*)

May 25

> *"You are never given a wish without also being given the power to make it come true. You may have to work for it, however."*
> —Richard Bach

May 26 1934 Sheila Greenwald

> *"More people should use their library."*
> —Regis Philbin (Who Wants to Be a Millionaire?, May 2, 2000)

Tip: Ask your local fast food restaurant for coupons for free french fries or other food items. The restaurants will usually give you enough for every student and staff member. Use these as thank you gifts to people who have all their library materials turned in at the end of the year. Have a grand prize for the class who has all their materials turned in first.

May 27

1907   Rachel Carson
1932   M.E. Kerr

> *"Read as you taste fruit or savor wine, or enjoy friendship, love or life."*
> —*Holbrook Jackson (1874–1948)*

May 28

*Describe the best teacher you ever had. How can you adapt that person's positive traits and use them in your professional practice?

> *"The failure to read good books both enfeebles the vision and strengthens our most fatal tendency — the belief that the here and now is all there is."*
> —*Allan Bloom*

May 29 1839 Mary L. Molesworth
1928 Willo Davis Roberts
1906 Terence Hanbury White

> *"What is reading but silent conversation?"*
> —Walter Savage Landor
> *(1775–1864)*

May 30 1912 Millicent Selsam

*What do you like to do in your free time? Have you been setting aside time for outside interests?

> *"It is no more necessary that a man should remember the different dinners and suppers which have made him healthy, than the different books which have made him wise. Let us see the results of good food in a strong body, and the results of great reading in a full and powerful mind."*
> —Sydney Smith *(1771–1845)*

Tip: Our school district uses popular book characters in the menus planned during National Library Week (e.g. Peter Rabbit Carrot stick or Alice salad). I display the books mentioned on the menu in the cafeteria. We have trivia questions each day from the books on display. Students received prizes of popular CD's, disks, reading posters, books, money, and ice cream.
—Rosa L. James-Alston, Bruton High School, Williamsburg, Virginia (Library Talk January/February 2001)

May 31 1893 Elizabeth Coatsworth
　　　　　　1914 Jay Williams

> *"Where any nation starts awake / Books are the memory. And it's plain / Decay of libraries is like / Alzheimer's in the nation's brain."*
> —*Ted Hughes,* Hear It Again

June

"What is one to say about June, / the time of perfect young summer, / the fulfillment of / the promise of the earlier months, / and with as yet no sign to remind one / that its fresh young beauty will ever fade."
—*Gertrude Jekyll*

Father's Day is this month

June 1 1889 James Daugherty
　　　　　　1878 John Masefield
　　　　　　1934 Doris Buchanan Smith

Tip: A quick way to shape behavior of kids in the elementary school library is to use cue words and phrases. One that works well for me is "Gimme Five." When giving your orientation at the beginning of the year, tell students that these are five behaviors you want them to exhibit when you hold up your hand, one for each finger. These can be such things as stop talking, listen, give me eye contact, put your pencil/pen/crayons down/put your hands in your lap, or other behaviors. I tell the students that when I hold up my hand from then on, I want them to do those five things, or "Gimme Five." Pretty soon, all I need to do to get the behavior I desire is just hold up my hand.
　　—*Donna Miller, Mesa County Valley School District #51, Grand Junction, Colorado (Library Talk May/June 2001)*

June 2 1929 Norton Juster
1938 Helen Oxenbury
1914 Paul Galdone

> "To read without reflecting is like eating without digesting."
> —Edmund Burke

Tip: Try this simple and effective technique to calm a noisy class. Say to them, "If you can hear me, raise your hand." One by one the students will raise their hands and stop talking. For younger students, move near a quiet child and say, "If you can hear me, clap once." Then move to another child. Pretty soon the noisy children quiet down.
—Mary Ziller, Potter Thomas Elementary School, Philadelphia, Pennsylvania (Library Talk March/April 2001)

June 3 1934 Anita Lobel

> "Finish each day and be done with it. You have done what you could. Some blunders and absurdities no doubt crept in, forget them as soon as you can. Tomorrow is a new day, you shall begin it well and serenely..."
> —Ralph Waldo Emerson

Tip: "Casey at the Bat" first appeared in The San Francisco Examiner on June 3, 1888. Read the poem as a class skit.

June 4

*Next year, I am going to be sure to . . .

> *"It often requires more courage to read some books than it does to fight a battle."*
> —*Sutton Elbert Griggs (1872–1930)*

Tip: Before you leave at the end of the day, get everything ready to make coffee or tea first thing in the morning. That way, it can be brewing while you are turning on all the computers and be ready for you when you need it!

June 5
1919 Richard Scarry
1929 Irene Haas

> *"There are books so alive that you're always afraid that while you weren't reading, the book has gone and changed, has shifted like a river; while you went on living, it went on living too, and like a river moved on and moved away. No one has stepped twice into the same river. But did anyone ever step twice into the same book?"*
> —*Marina Tsvetaeva*

Tip: Label scissors, staplers, and tape dispensers with permanent marker that say "IMC" or "Library." People borrow these all the time and forget where they got them.

Journal Pages

June 6 1911 Verna Aardema
1892 Will James
1954 Cynthia Rylant
1927 Peter Spier

> "A good library is a palace, a palace where the lofty spirits of all nations and generations meet."
> —Samuel Niger
> (1883–1956)

June 7 1943 Nicki Giovanni
1908 John Goodall

> "The roots of education are bitter, but the fruit is sweet."
> —Aristotle

Tip: Need to keep track of computer use figures and also track which patrons used which computers? Excel is an excellent tool to track each day's transactions. Use a single spreadsheet for each month. Each column records a day's transactions. When students come to the library to use the computers, have them pick up a slip with a computer station number on it, and scan their ID card with your barcode reader. The barcode number will be recorded in the spreadsheet cell. Because most barcodes have an embedded "enter" command, the cursor drops to the next cell in the column where you input the computer station number. At regular intervals include a time stamp (Control. Shift, Colon). It is easy at the end of the day to see how many computers were used. Simply divide the last row number by two. And you can search by computer number if you need to see the usage history for a specific computer.

—David Borgardus, Diamond Ranch High School, Pomona, California (**The Book Report** January/February 2002)

June 8 1921 Ivan Southall

> "A man will turn over half a library to make one book."
> —Samuel Johnson, Life of Johnson, *From James Boswell, April 6, 1775.*

Tip: Color code your file folders into four areas: library administration, collection, instruction, and other. Use one color for each area. It is easy to see at a glance which drawer the folder came from.

June 9

> "Learning is a treasure that will follow its owner everywhere."
> —Chinese Proverb

Journal Pages *81*

June 10 1925 Nat Hentoff
1928 Maurice Sendak

> "A great library contains the diary of the human race."
> —George Mercer Dawson, address on opening the Birmingham Free Library

Tip: Always perform some kind of work when talking on the phone: clean off a section of your desk, sort mail, organize a drawer, or do some other quick task.

June 11 1945 Robert Munsch

*Do you agree or disagree with this quote? How do you see yourself and your role as media specialist in relation to this quote?

> "While art, music, and P.E. are discipline areas, the school library media program is a resource and service agency and the school library media specialist is a resource and service person."
> —Barron/Bergen, Phi Delta Kappan

June 12
1819   Charles Kingsley
1827   Johanna Spryi

*Who is your biggest supporter on the staff? Why is that person so supportive?

> "I always dreamed you'd be my library buddy."
> (The Simpsons *episode*. Line spoken by the character of Lisa Simpson)

Tip: Examine your video/DVD collection. Are all your copies copyright compliant? Do you have off the air copies that should have been destroyed? Do any tapes need to be replaced? Is the content accurate? Are some tapes not being used? Put a list of current videos/DVDs in teachers' boxes so they know what is in the collection.

June 13
1962   Alexandra Sheedy

> "No one can make you feel inferior without your consent."
> —Eleanor Roosevelt

June 14 Flag Day
    1928   Janice May Udry
    1948   Laurence Yep
    1939   Penelope Farmer
    1811   Harriet Beecher Stowe

> "Any good history book is mainly just a long list of mistakes, complete with names and dates. It's very embarrassing."
> —Whitney Brown

Tip: Put a hand-written note in a teacher's box or send an e-mail message when you receive a new item that you think he/she would like to use. Ask them to respond to you with a note in your box or via e-mail indicating whether they would like to check out the item. Then, have the item delivered to their classroom for immediate use.

June 15   1939   Brian Jacques

> "A child becomes an adult when he realizes that he has a right not only to be right but also to be wrong."
> —Thomas Szasz

June 16
1897 Zachary Ball
1920 Isabelle Holland

> "We cannot have good libraries until we first have good librarians—properly educated, professionally recognized, and fairly rewarded."
> —Herbert S. White, Library Journal

June 17
1871 James Weldon Johnson

*When is your favorite time of your work day? Why do you like this time the best?

> "The art of reading is to skip judiciously."
> —Philip Gilbert Hamerton (1834–1894)

Tip: Provide a storybook snack with some of the books you share at story time. For example, most children today have never had the rice pudding or sarsaparilla mentioned in **Stuart Little**.

June 18
1942 Pat Hutchins
1949 Chris Van Allsburg

*If you were principal of your school, what would you change?

> "The reader cannot create; that has been done for him by the author. The reader can only interpret, giving the author a fair chance to make his impression."
> —Robertson Davies
> (1913–1995)

_____
_____
_____
_____
_____
_____

Tip: Don't feel bad saying "no" to requests for your time that will just add extra stress to your life. You will not be effective if you spread yourself too thin.

June 19

*What is the best way to treat people who are negative?

> "Everybody is ignorant, only on different subjects."
> —Will Rogers

_____
_____
_____
_____
_____
_____

Tip: Do you have a task or a project you have been putting off? Set a kitchen timer for 15 minutes. Then work as fast as you can on that task. Do not look at the timer or the clock—the bell will let you know when your time is up. You will be surprised at how much you can get done in 15 minutes when you really focus on a task. Once you have a good start on a project, it is not as difficult to go back to it later and finish.

June 20

> "In schools with good resource centers and the services of a teacher-librarian, students perform significantly better on tests for basic research skills. The evidence is similarly clear that more reading is done where there is a school library and a teacher-librarian."
> —Ken Haycock, "Competencies for Teacher-Librarians in the 21st Century," Teacher-Librarian

June 21 1925 Robert Kraus
1921 Patricia Wrightson

> "People say that life is the thing, but I prefer reading."
> —Logan Pearsall Smith (1865–1946)

Tip: Ask permission first, and then put photos of various teachers on your bulletin board along with a list of their favorite authors. Variation: Provide the title of each teacher's favorite children's book, fiction book, nonfiction book, favorite Web site, favorite software program, favorite subject in school, or other personal favorites.

June 22   1844   Margaret Sidney

*When have you received "a kick in the teeth"? What did you learn from the experience?

> "You may not realize it when it happens, but a kick in the teeth may be the best thing in the world for you."
> —Walt Disney

June 23   1924   Theodore Taylor

> "I've always tried to be aware of what I say in my films, because all of us who make motion pictures are teachers—teachers with very loud voices."
> —George Lucas

June 24   1909   Betty Cavanna
1916   John Ciardi
1924   Leonard Everett Fisher

> *"READ."*
> —*Caption on the ALA graphics posters*

Tip: Take photos of all of your library aides with a digital camera, then use the photos as wallpaper on your computers.
—*Anitra Gordon, Lincoln High School, Ypsilanti, Michigan (*The Book Report *May/June 2002)*

June 25   1892   Pearl Buck
1929   Eric Carle
1910   Elizabeth Orton Jones
1937   Jane Sarnoff

> *"Reading is seeing by proxy."*
> —*Herbert Spencer (1820–1903)*

Tip: Think really hard before you file something. Most of the things people file away in a cabinet are never looked at again. Is this something you really need to save or could you find this information again

June 26   1915   Charlotte Zolotow

*I wish I could learn . . . then I . . .

> "The mere brute pleasure of reading—the sort of pleasure a cow must have in grazing."
> —Gilbert K. Chesterton (1874–1936)

June 27   1880   Helen Keller
1936   Lucille Clifton

*It is important to balance your work life with your personal life. Are you taking time to enjoy your favorite hobbies? What is something in your personal life you would like to spend more time doing?

> "The marvelous richness of human experience would lose something of rewarding joy if there were no limitations to overcome. The hilltop hour would not be half so wonderful if there were no dark valleys to traverse."
> —Helen Keller (1880–1968)

June 28

> "Children are the living messages we send to a time we will not see."
> —*Neil Postman*, **The Disappearance of Childhood**

Tip: Reward student library assistants by letting them take a break with their favorite magazine. Let them be the first to read the new issues.

June 29   1900   Antoine Sainte-Exupery

> "A love affair with knowledge will never end in heartbreak."
> —*Michael Garrett Marino*

June 30
- 1922 Mollie Hunter
- 1904 Eleanor F. Lattimore
- 1940 David McPhail

> *"People who are resting on their laurels are wearing them on the wrong end."*
> —Malcolm Kushner

July

> "A summer breeze feels like a sigh
> And summer's days are long and warm
> Almost every garden in July
> Is rich with color, scent and form."
> —David Squire

July 1   1935   Leisel Skorpen

*What things do you think are beautiful? How can you bring this beauty into the library?

Tip: To make the Dewey Decimal System more relevant, I tell the origin of the system and then, dividing the 10 nonfiction areas into three parts, I spend three weeks reading interesting snippets from sample books. The children learn where to find these books in their own library and in any library, and they want to check them out immediately.
—*Lois Weems, Wildwood Elementary School, Sarcoxie, Missouri (Library Talk September/October 2001)*

July 2
1951 Jack Gantos
1919 Jean Craighead George

*What talents do you have? How are these talents important to who you are?

_____
_____
_____
_____
_____
_____
_____

> *"I write for children. Children are still in love with the wonders of nature, and I am too. So I tell them stories about a boy and a falcon, a girl and an elegant wolf pack, about owls, weasels, foxes, prairie dogs, the alpine tundra, the tropical rain forest. And when the telling is done, I hope they will want to protect all the beautiful creatures and places."*
> —Jean Craighead George

July 3

_____
_____
_____
_____
_____
_____

Tip: To help early primary students begin to explore information books without being completely overwhelmed by a large nonfiction section, select a few of the simpler nonfiction books from several high-interest subject areas and place colored dots just below the call number. House these books on an "Info to Grow" cart adjacent to the Picture Books. We keep them in Dewey order on the cart and have colorful number/picture labels on the cart shelves. The students really enjoy having easy access to these appealing nonfiction books.
—Janie Schomberg, Leal Elementary School Library, Urbana, Illinois (*Library Talk* May/June 2001)

July 4 Independence Day!
1933 Jamie Gilson
1804 Nathaniel Hawthorne

> "A library book... is not, then, an article of mere consumption but fairly of capital, and often in the case of professional men, setting out in life, is their only capital."
> —Thomas Jefferson
> (1743–1826)

July 5

> "Even in fiction writing, you shouldn't have anything that isn't necessary. Every word should be thought over. It's insulting to the reader for that writer to suppose that the reader wants to hear every work that pops into your head."
> —Carolyn Chute

July 6 1890   Dhan Gopal Mukerji
         1930   Gloria Skurzynski

*What is the area of greatest need in your library?
How are you going to address this problem?

_____
_____
_____
_____
_____
_____
_____
_____

July 7 1907   Robert A. Heinlein

_____
_____

> *"Literature remains the unexcelled means of interior exploration and connection-making."*
> *—Sven Birkerts, "The Gutenberg Elegies"*

_____
_____
_____
_____
_____
_____

Tip: Have one place and one place only that you keep keys for the library. Do not put them in your jacket pocket, or set them down "just for now." Countless hours are lost each year by people looking for keys!

July 8

> "Two forces are successfully influencing the education of a cultivated man: art and science. Both are united in the book."
> —Maksim Gorky (1868–1936)

July 9

Tip: Like most school librarians, I have trouble getting some of my high school students to return overdue library materials. For long overdues, I call the students down to the library and ask them if they have an answering machine at home. Most students do, so I have them call home and leave themselves a message to return the library materials. It works better than a letter to parents and most students have fun talking to themselves on the machine.
—Christine Nowicki, Montoursville (Pennsylvania) Area High School (The Book Report May/June 2002)

July 10 1937 Judie Angell
1792 Frederick Marryat

Tip: Before doing a Reader's Theatre presentation with a group, I use clip art from the computer to make signs for each character. I laminate the signs for durability, punch holes in the top, and thread yarn through the holes so the sign can be loosely hung around the student's neck. While Reader's Theatre is usually performed with few or no props, this enables the audience to remember which character is speaking. This is particularly important when there are several characters. The signs are then stored with the scripts for future use.
—*Laren Mench, Lake Ridge Academy, North Ridgeville, Ohio* (Library Talk *March/April 2001*)

July 11 1936 Helen Cresswell
1929 James Stevenson
1899 E. B. White

*Are you discouraged or concerned about something in your library program? What is not working the way you hoped it would? How can you work to change it?

> *"Being defeated is often a temporary condition. Giving up is what makes it permanent."*
> —*Marlene Savant*

July 12   1827   Johanna Spyri
               1909   Herbert Zim

> "A democratic society depends upon an informed and educated citizenry."
> —Thomas Jefferson
> (1743–1826)

July 13   1918   Marcia Brown

*What do you want your collection to look like in five years? What steps are needed for you to achieve this goal?

> "All the best stories in the world are but one story in reality—the story of escape. It is the only thing which interests us all and at all times, how to escape."
> —Arthur Christopher Benson

Tip: It is easy to let certain pieces of paperwork stay on your desk forever while you put them off over and over again. Each time you pick up a piece of paper, mark a dot in the upper right-hand corner. When you see you have looked at the same piece of paper three times, it is time to make a decision about it—it is taking up too much of your time.

July 14 1921 Leon Garfield
1927 Peggy Parish
1904 Isaac Bashevis Singer

> *"Information is the currency of democracy."*
> —Thomas Jefferson
> (1743–1826)

July 15 1903 Walter Edmonds
1779 Clement C. Moore

> *"If A equals success, then the formula is: A=X+Y+Z. X is work. Y is play. Z is keep your mouth shut."*
> —Albert Einstein

July 16 1935 Arnold Adoff

> "A popular government without popular information, or the means of acquiring it, is but a prologue to a farce or a tragedy, or perhaps both. Knowledge will forever govern ignorance, and a people who mean to be their own governors must arm themselves with the power which knowledge gives."
> —James Madison

Tip: Demonstrating a "can do" attitude will win many friends for your library and, hopefully, yourself. When someone asks you to do something that you cannot do for him or her, have a backup or optional item that you "can do" for him or her. Example: "We really can't check out all of the books on American Presidents to one teacher for the entire year, but here's what we 'can do.' When you are within a month of teaching that unit, let me know, and I will borrow books on presidents from other schools in the district. You will then have a very large collection in your classroom for use during the entire two weeks of your unit!"

July 17 1932 Karla Kuskin

> "Every time you stop a school, you will have to build a jail. What you gain at one end you lose at the other. It's like feeding a dog on his own tail. It won't fatten the dog."
> —Mark Twain

July 18

*What do you like most about yourself? Why are you like this?

_____

_____

_____

_____

> "The public library has been historically a vital instrument of democracy and opportunity in the United States.... Our history has been greatly shaped by people who read their way to opportunity and achievements in public libraries."
> —Arthur Meier Schlesinger (1888–1965)

Tip: *Instead of the same old desktop patterns, we set the computers to pictures of different places in the United States and make a monthly contest out of guessing the locations. To start, we kept it simple and used easily identifiable places such as the Grand Canyon, Niagara Falls, or The White House.. Students fill in the locations on a piece of paper and correct entries are put into a drawing for prizes. This desktop lesson is something fun for the students that could be expanded to other topics (places in the world, animals, famous people, whatever). It could even tie in with a unit of study.*
—Jane Carlson, Siskiyou County Office of Education, Austin, Minnesota (The Book Report September/October 2002)

July 19   1916   Eve Merriam
             1713   John Newbery

*What is something about which you feel sad?

> "Life is like an onion; you peel off one layer at a time, and sometimes you weep."
> —Carl Sandburg

_____

_____

_____

_____

_____

_____

_____

_____

_____

July 20

> "[Book collecting] is a curious mania instantly understood by every other collector and almost incomprehensible to the uncontaminated."
> —*Louis Auchincloss, A Writer's Capital*

July 21   1913   Catherine Storr

> "Of all the diversions of life, there is none so proper to fill up its empty spaces as the reading of useful and entertaining authors."
> —*Joseph Addison*

Tip: To remove the adhesive residue left by stickers on book jackets, spray a little Citrus Magic, or other popular citrus-oil product, on the sticky spot and wipe. This not only cleans the area but also makes it smell fresh. Use Spray and Wash to combat the sticky places on desks or wooden closet doors where posters were hung with masking tape.
—Sue Popjoy, M.T. Reilly Elementary School, Dallas, Texas (*The Book Report* November/December 2002)

July 22　1881　Margery W. Bianco

> "My grandma always said that God made libraries so that people didn't have any excuse to be stupid."
> —Joan Bauer

July 23　1926　Patricia Coombs
　　　　　1929　Robert Quackenbush

*What is something you are pessimistic about?

> "The absence of alternatives clears the mind marvelously."
> —Henry Kissinger

Tip: Meet with the local public children's librarian. Let her know of research units your students will be doing. Together you can discuss joint projects you both might want to do such as author visits, grant writing, and other projects.

July 24

> "I cannot think of a greater blessing than to die in one's own bed, without warning or discomfort, on the last page of the new book that we most wanted to read."
> —John Russell (1919–)

Tip: Use e-mail folders to sort your e-mail and keep your inbox empty.

July 25   1911   Ruth Krauss

*What signs could be made that would make the library easier to use?

> "This problem, too, will look simple after it is solved."
> —Charles Franklin Kettering

July 26 1945 Steven Cosgrove

*What is your favorite place in your library and why?

> "We should read to give our souls a chance to luxuriate."
> —Henry Miller (1891–1980)

Tip: We have our student helpers follow a particular method when shelving books: we ask that they place books pages-side down on the shelf, so that the books spine's are facing up and are parallel with the floor. Then we check the shelves. Using this method makes it easy to spot the books that were just shelved. If a book is in the right place, we stand it up properly. If not, it's taken back to the book cart and the student reshelves it. If there's a persistent problem with the helper's work, we go to the shelves with that student and demonstrate how the books should be shelved. Then we have the student shelve while we watch, and we offer help if it's needed.
—Mary Drexler, JCB High School, Phoenix, New York (The Book Report September/October 2002)

July 27 1870 Hillaire Belloc
1913 Scott Corbett

> "Just the knowledge that a good book is awaiting one at the end of a long day makes that day happier."
> —Kathleen Norris

July 28 1932 Natalie Babbitt
1866 Beatrix Potter

> *"The gears of poverty, ignorance, hopelessness and low self-esteem interact to create a kind of perpetual failure machine that grinds down dreams from generation to generation. We all bear the cost of keeping it running. Illiteracy is its linchpin."*
> —*Carl Sagan*

July 29 1869 Booth Tarkington

*List seven words that would describe your library. Which of these words would you like to change in the future?

> *"Experience is a hard teacher because she gives the test first, the lesson afterward."*
> —*Vernon Law*

106 *Day by Day: Professional Journaling for Library Media Specialists*

July 30

July 31 1929 Lynn Reid Banks
1930 Robert Kimmel Smith
1965 J. K. Rowling

*What makes your library magical? What entices patrons to enter the doors? What helps them to select a book that will transport them to another place and time?

"He had been so busy getting away from the library, he hadn't paid attention to where he was going."
—*J.K. Rowling*, **Harry Potter and the Sorcerer's Stone**

Tip: If your students enjoy the Harry Potter books, use a Potter theme to teach sorting. During a solemn ceremony, read the sorting hat song from J.K. Rowling's first book. The children select a piece of colored paper from the wizard's hat: Red for Gryffindor, yellow for Hufflepuff, blue for Ravenclaw, and green for Slytherin. Teachers get short forms to award points for good behavior and academic achievements — just like in Harry Potter books! Students bring the form to the library and place it in a specially marked basket, so it can be tallied at the end of the day. You can make this practice part of a Parents as Reading Partners program where children also receive points for turning in their reading records on time.
—*Kate Lallier, Robert W. Carbonara School, Valley Stream, New York* (**Library Talk** *November/December 2000*)

August

"If a cold August follows a hot July,
It foretells a winter hard and dry."
—*Unknown*

August 1

_____

_____

Tip: If you sometimes receive phone calls (such as tech or automation support) that can't be interrupted, print a variety of short, polite messages in bold fonts on bright paper and laminate them. Attach these to ping-pong paddles (which can be purchased at garage sales) or to a large paint stick. Drill a hole in the handle of the ping-pong paddle or stick, thread with a string or leather thong, and hang near the phone for instant courtesy. Then when you're in the middle of a call that you can't interrupt, you can grab a paddle and wave it at your would-be interruption like a virtuous picket sign. Best accompanied by a smile.
—*Sheryl Fullner, Nooksack Valley Middle School, Everson, WA (Library Talk September/October 2001)*

August 2
1924 James Baldwin
1900 Holling C. Holling
1946 James Howe

"You don't have to burn books to destroy a culture. Just get people to stop reading them."
—*Ray Bradbury (1920–)*

*What is something you dislike about yourself and would like to change?

_____
_____
_____
_____
_____
_____

Tip: Write a welcome back to school note to your staff. Include an AV check-out list and an invitation to set up a time to plan together.

108 *Day by Day: Professional Journaling for Library Media Specialists*

August 3
1926 Mary Calhoun
1841 Juliana Horatio Ewing

*What was your favorite picture book as a child? Why was it special to you?

> "A healthy attitude is contagious but don't wait to catch it from others. Be a carrier."
> —Unknown

Tip: Consider adding some bookstore touches to your library, such as scattered seating in wingback chairs with reading lamps nearby.

August 4

> "A house without books is like a room without windows. No man has a right to bring up children without surrounding them with books... Children learn to read being in the presence of books."
> —Heinrich Mann
> (1871–1950)

Tip: Make a list of AV equipment that needs to be purchased this year. Schedule a time for you to obtain bids and to write up purchase orders.

August 5
1902	Robert Bright
1889	Maud Petersham
1880	Ruth Sawyer

> "The price of greatness is responsibility."
> —Winston Churchill

*What are your top three priorities that you need to keep in mind to create a successful library?

___

Tip: If your library wins an award or is honored in some way, have a banner made at a sign shop and hang it near the entrance of the library. Also, let the local newspaper know about it.

August 6
1917	Matt Christopher
1917	Barbara Cooney

> "Children's books are written for upbringing... but upbringing is a great thing; it decides the fate of the human being."
> —Vissarion Grigor'evich Belinskii (1811–1841)

___

Tip: Don't play telephone tag: when you leave a message for someone, leave a detailed one so they don't have to call you back or they will call back with what you needed. This eliminates back and forth calling. Always leave your phone number and repeat it twice.

August 7
- 1928 Betsy Byars
- 1927 Maia Wojciechowska

> "The pleasure of reading is doubled when one lives with another who shares the same books."
> —Katherine Mansfield (1888–1923)

Tip: Before helpers arrive, take five books from the shelving cart (Choose a wide variety of the most difficult.) and hold them so that their spines all face down. Photocopy the five spines at once. Keep a photocopy on your desk and after the suspect shelver has come and gone, check the whereabouts of those books. If there are any problems, pull the books and discuss the fine points with the helper whose name you put on the photocopy along with the date. Make sure this is not an accusatory conference. It should be more along the lines of, "I've noticed you have a little difficulty with double digit decimals. Let's see if we can make a cheat sheet to help you." The review is helpful, but those little words "I've noticed" coupled with the actual photocopy helps folks know that accountability is required.
—Sheryl Kindle Fullner, Nooksack Valley Middle School, Everson, Washington (The Book Report *March/April 2002*)

August 8
- 1936 Jan Pienkowski
- 1896 Marjorie K. Rawlings

Tip: When our school held its homecoming weekend, I asked the eight homecoming court girls and their escorts to bring in a 5 by 7 picture of themselves (Most had had their senior picture taken.) and to tell me their favorite library book. The court's photos and accompanying books were featured in the lobby display case. Information about the book was featured daily on the morning announcements. It was a great promotion for the students, the library, and reading!
—Christine Nowicki, Montoursville Area High School, Montoursville, Pennsylvania (The Book Report *November/December 2002*)

August 9
- 1914 Tove Jansson
- 1944 Patricia McKissack

> "Only a generation of readers will spawn a generation of writers."
> —Steven Spielberg (1947–)

August 10
- 1917 Margot Tomes

> "New Laws of Librarianship: Libraries serve humanity. Respect all forms by which knowledge is communicated. Use technology intelligently to enhance service. Protect free access to knowledge. Honor the past & create the future."
> —Michael Gorman
> (American Libraries September 1995)

August 11
- 1897 Enid Blyton
- 1908 Don Freeman

*What are your big dreams for your library? If time and money were not hurdles, what would you change about your library?

> "We think too small. Like the frog at the bottom of the well, he thinks the sky is only as big as the top of the well. If he surfaced, he would have an entirely different view."
> —Mao Tse-Tung

August 12
- 1923 Ruth Stiles Gannett
- 1946 Deborah Howe
- 1937 Walter Dean Myers

*What is your most indispensable item at work and why is it so important?

> "I am what the librarians have made me with a little assistance from a professor of Greek and a few poets."
> —Bernard Keble Sandwell, Quoted by J.R. Kidd in *Learning and Society*

Tip: Each month highlight a different grade level or department at your school. Make a display with teachers' pictures and show books the teachers enjoy or books that go along with the subject matter they teach. Create a trivia card for each teacher. "Did you know that: Mrs. Larsen was born in Denver, collects Pez dispensers, loves to paint, Little House in the Big Woods was the first novel she read, loves to travel, her favorite picture book is Polar Express, and she almost cut off her earlobe when she was seven years old! Kids and adults alike will enjoy these displays, and it will help the staff members feel connected to the library.

August 13
1845	Walter Crane
1915	Brinton Turkle
1823	Charlotte Yonge

August 14

> "The richest minds need not large libraries."
> —*Amos Bronson Alcott*

August 15   1858   Edith Nesbit

*The next time . . . . . happens with a teacher, I am going to . . . . .

_____
_____
_____
_____
_____
_____

> *"He that loves a book will never want a faithful friend, a wholesome counselor, a cheerful companion, an effectual comforter. By study, by reading, by thinking, one may innocently divert and pleasantly entertain himself, as in all weathers, as in all fortunes."*
> —Barrow

Tip: Schedule your book fairs early in the school year while there are still days available from the book fair company. Better yet, schedule them in the spring for the next school year. It is a good idea to schedule the book fair for dates where most of your parents will be at school such as Back to School Night, Conferences, Chili Supper, or other schoolwide event.

August 16   1909   Marchette Chute
             1914   Beatrice S. DeRegniers

_____
_____
_____
_____
_____
_____
_____
_____
_____
_____

August 17
- 1937 Ariane Dewey
- 1926 Myra Cohn Livingston
- 1863 Gene Stratton Porter

*What have you had to let go of in your position as a library media specialist? How did that affect you?

> "There's an important difference between giving up and letting go."
> —Jessica Hatchigan

August 18
- 1944 Paula Danziger
- 1904 Louise Fatio

*If you had an extra hour each day, what would you do with it?

> "Go ahead and do the impossible. It's worth the look on the faces of those who said you couldn't."
> —Walter Bagehot

August 19 1902 Ogden Nash

*What makes you laugh?

> "Copy from one, it's plagiarism; copy from two, it's research."
> —Wilson Mizner
> (1876–1933)

August 20

> "Teaching students how to find information rather than memorize information was ranked highest in importance in this year's Association for Supervision and Curriculum Development (ASCD) Issues Survey." Teaching students how to find information has always been the goal of the school library media specialist.
> —Education Update, 42, January 2000.

Journal Pages 117

August 21

Tip: Use cue words and phrases with children. Example: Instead of saying, "Be quiet, look at me, put your pencils down, and listen," teach the behaviors you want, then use a cue phrase such as "listening position" to get that behavior.

August 22

*What are you worried about? What could cause problems for your library program in the future?

> *"In science, read by preference the newest works. In literature, read the oldest. The classics are always modern."*
> —Lord Edward Lytton
> (1803–1873)

August 23

> "How can you sit down to write until you have stood up to live?"
> —Henry David Thoreau

Tip: During a recent library visit to find information for biology projects, ninth and tenth grade students had the opportunity to participate in a peer teaching activity. Before students arrived, we prepared activity sheets for each of the library's online subscription databases. The sheets listed a series of tasks to practice, using suggested "successful" search terms, and were designed to highlight the special strength of each database. Students worked in groups of two or three and practiced the search tasks on their assigned databases for about 10 minutes. The groups then demonstrated the basic use of each database while "broadcasting" their searches from the teaching station to the rest of the class. Students were actively engaged in the process and enjoyed their teaching experiences, while learning about the databases from each other.
—Sandy McLukie, Episcopal High School Library, Jacksonville, Florida (The Book Report May/June 2002)

August 24

*At the beginning of the day, I felt . . .
Now I feel . . . The reason for this change (or status quo) is . . .

> "It requires a very unusual mind to undertake an analysis of the obvious."
> —A. A. Whitehead

August 25

> *"To feel most beautifully alive means to be reading something beautiful, ready always to apprehend in the flow of language the sudden flash of poetry."*
> —Gaston Bachelard

August 26   1922   Patricia Beatty

*What is welling up within you that you need to write about in your journal?

> *"I listen to myself, allow myself to be lead, not by anything on the outside, but by what wells up from within."*
> —Etty Hillesum

Tip: Introduce your new books each year (and promote the library) with a staff "Tea and Chocolate" after school near the beginning of the year. Divide all the new books into subject areas and display them invitingly. Then have a goodies table with a fancy punch and platters of rich chocolate. The teachers will be impressed that you fussed so much for them — and that you are buying for their specific curricula!
     —Ellen Bell, Amador Valley High School, Pleasanton, California (Library Talk May/June 2002)

August 27 1921   Arlene Mosel

*What kind of trophy or award would you like to see your library win?

___

Tip: Set up a bookmark-designing center in the library. Provide strips of colored paper, die cut outs if you have them, sticker, markers, and clear contact paper. This center can be used as a reward for students whenever the occasion calls for it. You can offer this center to teachers who might want to create bookmarks as rewards for their students. Another good use of the center is to create bookmarks to celebrate and promote special events such as National Library Week or Children's Book Week.

August 28
- 1904   Roger Duvoisin
- 1926   Phyllis Krasilovsky
- 1924   F.N. Monjo
- 1937   Allen Say
- 1915   Tasha Tudor

> "Reading—the best state yet to keep absolute loneliness at bay."
> —William Styron (1925–)

August 29 1952 Karen Hesse
1916 Joseph Jacobs

*What is the leadership style of your administrative team? Is it a good match for you?

> "When someone demands blind obedience, you'd be a fool not to peek."
> —Jim Fiebig

_____
_____
_____
_____

Tip: Save book jackets from laminated books to display as new books or for an author of the month (If the author or an artist visits, ask them to autograph the cover.), or for library lessons on authors and titles. You can also turn laminated book jackets into puzzles or bookmarks. Let students decorate lockers and cover textbooks with excess jackets. You could even create borders and columns on the library walls.
—Carol Kotsch, St. Elizabeth Ann Saton, Wichita, Kansas (The Book Report November/December 2002)

August 30 1925 Laurent de Brunhoff
1909 Virginia Lee Burton
1938 Donald Crews
1921 Sesyle Joslin
1797 Mary W. Shelley

*Who do you talk to when you have a problem? Why is this a good person with whom to share your problems?

> "If you have solved all the problems in your life, if you no longer ponder, then you're not a writer."
> —Doris Betts

_____
_____
_____
_____
_____
_____
_____

August 31

*There is a big difference between activity and productivity. How do you spend most of your day?

> "It's not enough to be busy. The question is: What are we busy about?"
> —Henry David Thoreau

_____
_____
_____
_____
_____

Tip: When deciding between two tasks, pick the one that will yield the greatest results for your program. For example, should you spend 45 minutes fixing a printer that has never worked correctly, or should you spend the same 45 minutes writing a grant for all new equipment?

September

" 'Tis the last rose of summer, / Left blooming alone; / All her lovely companions / Are faded and gone."
—Thomas Moore, "The Last Rose of Summer"

September is Library Card Sign-up Month.

Labor Day occurs in this month

September 1   1875   Edgar Rice Burroughs

*How do you feel on the first day of school? How do the students feel?

> "The most important day of a person's education is the first day of school, not Graduation Day."
> —Harry K. Wong

_____
_____
_____
_____
_____
_____

Journal Pages   *123*

September 2   1850   Eugene Field
1820   Lucretia Hale

> *"There is an art of reading, as well as an art of thinking, and an art of writing."*
> —Isaac D'Israeli
> (1766–1848)

September 3

> *"For whatever is truly wondrous and fearful in man, never yet was put into words or books."*
> —Herman Melville, **Moby Dick**

Tip: Collaborate with your local public librarian. The book fair company we use provides us with a costume of a favorite book character to promote the fair. We let the public library use the costume one morning for their preschool story time. In exchange, they pass out information about our book fair and invite preschool parents to visit the book fair. It is a win–win for both libraries!

September 4
1924   Joan Aiken
1912   Syd Hoff

*How do you maintain your sense of humor? What do you do to bring humor to others?

> *"Outside of a dog, a book is a man's best friend. Inside of a dog, it's too dark to read."*
> —Groucho Marx

_____
_____
_____
_____
_____
_____

Tip: Have kids submit their best jokes. Make sure you set the standards for appropriate jokes. Post the best ones in the library. Have a display of joke books available.

September 5
1952   Paul Fleischman

*What did you want to be when you were a child? How does this fit or not fit with being a librarian?

> *"No one can read with profit that which he cannot learn to read with pleasure."*
> —Noah Porter (1811–1892)

_____
_____
_____
_____
_____
_____

Tip: Put famous folks all around the library! On your Dewey posters for each section in the library, put a picture of a famous person who worked in that field. For example, have a picture of Neil Armstrong in the space travel section, Julia Child near the cookbooks. Show how each section ties into a career your students might want to pursue.

September 6   1869   Felix Salten

*If you could take five books on a deserted island with you for pleasure reading, what would you take?

> "My father gave me free run of his library. When I think of my boyhood, I think in terms of the books I read."
> —Jorge Luis Borges
> (1899–1986)

Tip: Schedule any author visits you want to have this year. They are not all expensive! Look for local authors and authors who may already be in town for another event. Contact local bookstores and see whom they are bringing into town. See if you can pair up with other libraries to share expenses.

September 7   1904   C. B. Colby

> "Be lions roaring through the forests of knowledge."
> —Baha'i Scriptures

September 8 National Pledge of Allegiance Day

1940   Jack Prelutsky

> "The true University of these days is a Collection of Books."
> —Thomas Carlyle, "The Hero as Man of Letters"

*What interview questions do you think should be asked of someone applying for a library job? How would you answer these questions?

_____
_____
_____
_____
_____

Tip: Block out times on your schedule to process your e-mail. Twice per day should be enough. Avoid the temptation to check e-mail more frequently.

September 9
1906   Aileen Fisher
1903   Phyllis Whitney

> "The art of reading is, among other things, the art of adopting that pace the author has set. Some books are fast and some are slow, but no book can be understood if it is taken at the wrong speed."
> —Mark Van Doren (1894–1973)

_____
_____
_____
_____

Tip: At the beginning of the school year, I hand out sheets of poster board cut in half vertically to groups of students. They are assigned a range of Dewey numbers such as 500–550 and given a glue stick along with a pile of old magazines. They go to an Internet site that describes Dewey numbers and then look for items to clip out to illustrate their numbers. Cooperative social and leadership skills come into play as they divide up the work. They print out large fancy numbers on the word processor and glue them near the pictures with the lowest number at the top as they work their way down the board. This project is more fun and cheaper than ordering Dewey posters for mounting on shelving endcaps or suspending from our ceiling on monofilament line.
    —Sheryl Kindle Fulner, Librarian, Nooksack Valley Middle School, Everson, Washington (The Book Report *September/October 2002*)

September 10 1916 Robert McClung

*What is your favorite book and why?

_____
_____
_____
_____
_____
_____
_____
_____

> "Ranganathan's Five Laws:
> Books are for use.
> Books are for all; or Every reader his book.
> Every book its reader.
> Save the time of the reader.
> A library is a growing organism."
> —Shiyali Ramamrita Ranganathan (1892–1972)

Tip: Let students check out every day. Once a week is not enough to visit the best room in the school!

September 11 1946 Anthony Browne
1926 Alfred Slote

*What are the top five priorities in your life? Does your time reflect these priorities?

_____
_____
_____
_____
_____
_____
_____

> "Terrorist attacks can shake the foundations of our biggest buildings, but they cannot touch the foundation of America. These acts shatter steel, but they cannot dent the steel of American resolve."
> —George W. Bush, President of the United States of America

Tip: Keep in mind that no matter how much you enjoy your job, it is still just a job. It is very easy to spend long hours after school instead of going home or taking piles of work home to do each night. Family should come first. If for some reason you were no longer able to perform your job, a replacement would be hired. But, if your family were to lose you, they would never again be the same.

128 Day by Day: Professional Journaling for Library Media Specialists

September 12

> "Library / Here is where people, / One frequently finds, / Lower their voices / And raise their minds."
> —Richard Armour, Light Armour

Tip: To learn kindergartners' names quickly, elicit response to literature, and make attractive take-home projects, take individual photos of kids holding large nametags. Use the photos to learn students' names during the first few weeks of school. Make a simple accordion-fold book, shaped like a worm, for each student. Have students make drawings after hearing stories. After several weeks, cut out the children's faces from the first-of-the-school photos. Glue each to the cover of a worm book. Glue student's drawings into its pages. Each "bookworm" has a record of stories "devoured."
—Loann Scarpato, Abington Friends Schools, Jenkintown, Pennsylvania (Library Talk January/February 2002)

September 13

1916 Roald Dahl
1917 Carol Kendall
1920 Else Minarik

*What do you remember school libraries were like when you were a child? How have they changed?

> "If your plan is for one year, plant rice; / If your plan is for ten years, plant trees; / If your plan is for a hundred years, / Educate children.
> —Confucius

Tip: As a library promotion, design a colorful bookmark for your library, with contact information, library logo, and a quote from a book. Or, as a contest, have classes compete for the best bookmark design, with the winner getting a free book or other suitable recognition. For long-lasting bookmarks, laminate them and add a tassel to a punched hole.
—Ava Goldman, California Public Employees' Retirement System, Sacramento, California (The Book Report March/April 2002)

September 14   1914   William H. Armstrong
　　　　　　　　　1910   Edith Thacher Hurd
　　　　　　　　　1950   John Steptoe

*My best friend on the staff is . . .
This is what I like about this person . . .

> "The only way to have a friend is to be one."
> —Ralph Waldo Emerson

_____
_____
_____
_____

September 15   1789   James Fenimore Cooper
　　　　　　　　　1914   Robert McCloskey
　　　　　　　　　1934   Tomie DePaola

*One area in which I plan to grow professionally this year is . . .

> "It is just sort of an accident that I write books. I really think up stories in pictures and just fill in between the pictures with a sentence or a paragraph or a few pages of words."
> —Robert McCloskey

_____
_____
_____
_____
_____
_____

Tip: You keep a desk pad calendar for class scheduling, but you don't memorize it. Why not make scheduling easier by keeping your media center schedule online? If your school Web site doesn't have room, try <myschoolonline.com>, a free Web site where you can set up such a calendar along with other information. You'll be able to go to any available computer and schedule on the spot.
　　—Robert L. Otte, South Christian High School, Grand Rapids, Michigan (*Library Talk* November/December 2001)

September 16 1898   H.A. Rey

> "A Library that is not accessible out of business hours is of as little value as gold hoarded in a vault and withdrawn from circulation."
> —Alexander Graham Bell, letter to Mabel Hubbard Bell, 17 November 1896

Tip: Change your computer passwords every so often. It is a good idea to have your passwords contain a variety of letters, numbers, and symbols.

September 17 1909   Elizabeth Enright

*How do other staff members perceive the library? Is their perception accurate? What can you do to increase their understanding of you and your program?

> "What concerns me is not the way things are, but rather the way people think things are."
> —Epictetus

Tip: Short on desk space? Hang a shoe bag on the back of your office door. Use the shoe slots to hold your stapler, tape, scissors, flashlight, and other items.

September 18

> "Any book that helps a child to form a habit of reading, to make reading one of his deep and continuing needs, is good for him."
> —Richard McKenna

Tip: The beginning of the school year is a good time to check all your AV equipment. Plug in each piece and make sure everything is working.

September 19

1938   Vicki Cobb
1894   Rachel Field
1867   Arthur Rackham

*If I were the superintendent, I would . . . .

> "We keep moving forward, opening up new doors, and doing new things, because we're curious and curiosity keeps leading us down new paths."
> —Walt Disney

Tip: The first Mickey Mouse cartoon was shown in New York on this day in 1928. Make a display of Disney books to commemorate that day!

September 20   1888   Miska Petersham

*What advice would you give a new student to your school?

> "A great teacher never strives to explain his vision. He simply invites you to stand beside him and see for yourself."
> —R. Inman

_____

_____

_____

Tip: Some paperwork is urgent, others can wait for a while. The problem is how to keep them handy and not let them get buried into the piles. Solution: Get three different colors of stacking letter trays.
- *Label the top one (I like to use a red tray.), "URGENT—Handle today!"*
- *Label the second tray, "Do By Friday" and*
- *Label the bottom tray, "Do By the 30th."*

This way your paper work will be turned in on time, and you can tell your priorities at a glance.

September 21   1866   H.G. Wells
                  1908   Taro Yashima

*What mistakes have you made? What lessons did you learn?

> "Mistakes are part of the dues one pays for a full life."
> —Sophia Loren

_____

_____

_____

_____

_____

Tip: If you have a display cabinet, have staff and students bring in their collections to share.

September 22   1908   Esphyr Slobodkina

> "Two more recent studies in Alaska and Pennsylvania also show a rise in test scores tied to school library resources and staffing."
> —Kathleen Manzo, "Study Shows Rise in Test Scores Tied to School Library Resources," *Education Week*

Tip: Look on the remnant table at the fabric store. If you can find one yard of a fabric you like, you have a display cloth! Either cut the edges with pinking shears or run a quick hem on the sewing machine and you are done. Look for prints that you can use for a particular theme (i.e., a dog print to display dog books, a red check for farm books). Place a small box under the cloth and you have created a two level display area.

September 23

*What has "always been done that way" in your library? Is it still effective? What changes need to be made?

> "The most damaging phrase in the language is: "It's always been done that way.""
> —Rear Admiral Grace Hopper

September 24

1898	Harry Behn
1932	Jane Curry
1913	Wilson Rawls

> "The object of teaching a child is to enable him to get along without his teacher."
> —Elbert Hubbard

Tip: Buy an accordion file labeled 1 through 31 and another one labeled with the months of the year from the office supply store. Put it in a file drawer at your desk area. When you get agendas for upcoming meetings or other upcoming events, place it in the correct 1 through 31 slot for meetings this month or file it in the monthly file for upcoming months.

September 25

> "If you didn't want them to think, you shouldn't have given them library cards."
> —Robert Kaufman, Getting Straight (Line spoken by Elliott Gould as Harry Bailey)

Tip: Invite neighborhood preschoolers in for a story time and a check-out time once or twice a month. Both kids and parents are more comfortable when that first day of kindergarten comes around.

September 26

*In order to improve communication with staff, I plan to . . .

___

Tip: When sending out communications, such as new book lists to teachers, I put a small bulb at the bottom that describes current school library research findings. This helps to promote the use of the library in the teaching and learning process among classroom teachers. For example, one item might read: Current research findings have revealed that students academic achievement is increased when collaborative planning between the classroom teacher and the school librarian occurs.
—Patricia L. Kolencik, North Clarion High School Library, Tionesta, Pennsylvania (Library Talk *January/February 2001*)

September 27   1933   Paul Goble
                                 1924   Bernard Waber

*Describe a student you enjoy working with. What characteristics does this student have that you admire?

"If you think education is expensive, try ignorance."
—Derek Bok, Harvard University President

September 28   1856   Kate Douglas Wiggin

> "I would be most content if my children grew up to be the kind of people who think decorating consists mostly of building enough bookshelves."
> —Anna Quindlen, "Enough Bookshelves," New York Times

Tip: When you send materials to a teacher's classroom, make a circulation card for each book. Include call number, author, and title on book cards of a color you don't use for library materials. (I use yellow.). Send the cards with the materials to the teacher, who can use them to keep track of students borrowing materials from the classroom. Keep the cards for future units. They are easier to update than a printed bibliography.
    —*Cathy Keim, Meadowbrook (Pennsylvania) School* (The Book Report *May/June 2001*)

September 29

> "To bring up a child in the way he should go, travel that way yourself once in awhile."
> —Henry Wheeler Shaw

Journal Pages *137*

September 30
1898   Edgar D'Aulaire
1916   Alvin Tresselt

*Look at the color scheme in the library. Is it appealing? Could a new accent color be added? How could out-of-date colors be eliminated or camouflaged?

> *"You see, I don't believe that libraries should be drab places where people sit in silence, and that's been the main reason for our policy of employing wild animals as librarians."*
> —Monty Python *skit*

_____
_____
_____
_____
_____

Tip: Do you have a pillar that is in an awkward place? Sponge paint it three shades of brown, paint in trunk lines, drill small holes near the top and place artificial Christmas tree branches in the holes. Add a park bench and you have created a cozy reading area out of an eyesore.

October

October is Read Aloud Month

> "October skips along the lanes.
> It kicks the leaves, and laughs with rains."
> —Inez Rice

October 1

_____
_____

> *"I quit school in the 5th grade because of pneumonia. Not because I had it, but because I couldn't spell it."*
> —Rocky Graziano

_____
_____
_____
_____

Tip: Are your dictionaries up-to-date? Dictionaries over 10 years old need to be replaced.

October 2

> *"In the book of life, the answers aren't in the back."*
> —Charlie Brown, Peanuts

Tip: The **Peanuts** *comic strip was first published in 1950. Make a display of Peanuts books. Have a contest to guess how many peanuts are in the jar.*

October 3

1906	Natalie Savage Carlson
1918	Molly Cone
1948	Marilyn Singer

> *"Reading is to the mind what exercise is to the body."*
> —Richard Steele

*Five years from now I want to be . . .

Tip: Study the layout of your library. Does traffic flow easily? Are there areas for large group activities as well as small group areas? If you were a stranger walking into this library, could you find what you need without asking? Is the layout intuitive? What do you want to keep and what would you like to change?

October 4

1916	Julia Cunningham
1892	Robert Lawson
1905	Munro Leaf
1924	Donald Sobol

> "I lived with them in my studio in New York. And of course if I were doing that book today or even ten years, fifteen years later, I would have gone to where the wild ducks were and where I could study them— I would have gone to the country somewhere."
> —Robert McCloskey

Tip: In Boston on this day in 1987, the Mallard Family Sculpture in honor of Robert McCloskey's story **Make Way for Ducklings**, was dedicated. Read it out loud to commemorate the event!

October 5

| 1928 | Louise Fitzhugh |
| 1913 | Gene Zion |

> "Nothing is more dangerous than an idea when it is the only one you have."
> —Emile Chartier

Tip: Start a Mother–Daughter Book Club. (Grandmothers are invited too!) A good book to start with is **Sarah, Plain and Tall** by Patricia Maclaughlin. It is a quick read and an interesting story for a variety of age levels.

Possible discussion questions could include:
- *What did the wagon symbolize in this story?*
- *Why did Caleb want Anna to keep telling the story of his birth over and over again?*
- *What responsibilities did Anna have to take on at a young age?*
- *Why did Jacob send away for a bride?*
- *Why did Sarah answer the ad?*
- *What risks were they both taking by meeting this way?*
- *Could this work today?*
- *What is a family? When did the people in this story become a family?*

October 6   1914   Thor Heyerdahl
　　　　　　　1919   Lee Kingman

*What do you do to greet patrons when they come into the library? How do you make them feel welcome?

> "A house without books is like a room without windows. No man has a right to bring up children without surrounding them with books.... Children learn to read being in the presence of books."
> —Heinrich Mann
> (1871–1950)

_____
_____
_____
_____
_____
_____
_____
_____
_____

October 7   1893   Alice Dalgliesh
　　　　　　　1942   Susan Jeffers
　　　　　　　1849   James Whitcomb Riley
　　　　　　　1929   Robert Westall

*In order to improve communication with parents, I plan to . . .

> "To read a writer is for me not merely to get an idea of what he says, but to go off with him and travel in his company."
> —André Gide

_____
_____
_____
_____
_____
_____
_____

Tip: Create thank you notes with your library logo and have several made up to have on hand. Write at least one thank you note a week to a student, parent, or other staff member.

October 8   1920   Barthe DeClements
1920   Frank Herbert
1925   Edward Ormondroyd
1943   R. L. Stine

> "Librarian is a service occupation. Gas station attendant of the mind."
> —Richard Powers, **The Gold Bug Variations**

Tip: This is Silly Day. Everyone needs one now and then. Write silly poems or stories or think up silly games. Maybe everyone could wear something silly.

October 9   1937   Johanna Hurwitz

> "One unquenchable longing has the mastery of me, which hitherto I neither would nor could repress; 'tis an insatiable craving for books, although, perhaps, I already have more than I ought."
> —Francesco Petrarch, in **Francesco Petrarca** by E.H.R. Tatham

Tip: Have a bedtime story time in the library one night for your younger patrons. Invite them and their parents to come to the library with their pajamas on and have cookies and milk and listen to a few wonderful bedtime stories. You can wear your robe and slippers too!

October 10   1942   James Marshall

*Why do patrons want to come to this library? What is inviting about this library?

> "My mother and my father were illiterate immigrants from Russia. When I was a child they were constantly amazed that I could go to a building and take a book on any subject. They couldn't believe this access to knowledge we have here in America. They couldn't believe that it was free."
> —Kirk Douglas (1916–)

Tip: We stirred a lot of students and faculty interest with our READ mini-posters (an ALA poster take-off) featuring our own students, teachers, staff and custodians photographed with their favorite books. We displayed the faculty and staff posters in the library and students' pictures on three bulletin boards. All we needed was a digital camera, computer and software, regular copy machine paper, and a laminating machine.
—Petty Gandolfo and Dee Parks, Madison Central High School, Richmond, Kentucky (The Book Report *May/June 2001*)

October 11   1929   Russell Freedman

*There will be people on your staff who love to play the games of "One Downmanship" and "Busier Than Thou." Have you gotten caught up in this bad habit? What can you do to avoid these conversations?

> "Man invented language to satisfy his deep need to complain."
> —Lily Tomlin

October 12

*What three words would describe you this week?

> "You must live feverishly in a library. Colleges are not going to do any good unless you are raised and live in a library every day of your life."
> —Ray Douglas Bradbury, **Writer's Digest**

Tip: Do your students have access to the local public library? Invite someone from the nearest public library and have him or her speak to groups of children about what the public library has to offer. Send home information about how to sign up for a library card. At Back to School night or conference night, have someone from the local public library come over and sign people up for library cards. We want our students to be life-long library users!

October 13   1902   Arna Bontemps

> "To acquire the habit of reading is to construct for yourself a refuge from almost all of the miseries of life."
> —W. Somerset Maugham (1874–1965)

Tip: Do something with every piece of paper that reaches you and put it in its proper place—not just back on the pile.

144 *Day by Day: Professional Journaling for Library Media Specialists*

October 14
1926 Miriam Cohen
1893 Lois Lenski

*What do you consider to be the best children's or young adults' books? How can you share them with students?

> "It does not matter how many books you may have, but whether they are good or not."
> —Lucius Annaeus Senec, Epistolae Morale

Tip: Create a Book Hospital cart for books that need mending. Let the students know about the hospital and soon they will be pointing out repairs that need to be made!

October 15

> "America's future walks through the doors of our schools each day."
> —Mary Jean Le Tendre

October 16

1900   Edward Ardizzone
1854   Oscar Wilde
1942   Joe Bruchac

> "Voluntary reading is the best predictor of reading comprehension, vocabulary growth, spelling ability, grammatical usage and writing style. Access to school library media centers results in more voluntary reading by students. Having a school library media specialist makes a difference in the amount of voluntary reading done."
> —Stephen Krashen, The Power of Reading

October 17   Black Poetry Day

> "Alone, all alone / Nobody, but nobody / Can make it out here alone."
> —Maya Angelou

October 18 1930 Nancy Winslow Parker

> *"Teaching consists of equal parts perspiration, inspiration and resignation."*
> —Susan Ohanian

Tip: Is your desk always cluttered with items you must keep at hand such as lesson plans, ordering information, and catalogs? Find a shelving unit to place in your work area. Get letter trays for each of your reoccurring piles. For example, have a letter tray for each grade level or subject area you work with, one for journals to be read, one for correspondence that must be answered, and one for catalogs you would like to look at. Now you have a vertical desk that doesn't take up valuable desk space!

October 19 1931 Ed Emberly

*How do you feel about your time management skills? What is working? What needs improvement?

> *"Work expands to fill the time available for its completion."*
> —C. Northcote Parkinson

October 20
1906 Crockett Johnson
1908 Wylly Folk St. John

*How can you make your schedule more flexible? Whose help will you need to enlist? What obstacles will you have to overcome?

> *"When flexibly scheduled, the teacher-librarian and resource center can have a significant effect on student achievement in information handling and use and in content areas. Indeed, the most significant changes in library programs occur when the teacher-librarian moves to flexible scheduling and curriculum-integrated instruction; positive cooperative relations with teachers, administrators, and students contribute to this success."*
> —Bishop, "The Roles of the School Library Media Specialist in an Elementary School using a Literature-Based Reading Program: an Ethnographic Case Study."

October 21
1929 Ursula LeGuin
1933 Polly Longsworth

*What steps have you taken to make your instructional program more collaborative? Which teachers on the staff would be the most open to collaboration? How could you approach them about collaborating? What resistance do you anticipate and how could you counteract it?

> *"Free every Monday through Friday—knowledge. Bring your own containers."*
> —E. C. McKenzie, Sign on a high school library's bulletin board in Dallas

October 22

> *"We shouldn't teach great books; we should teach a love of reading."*
> —B.F. Skinner
> (1904–1990)

October 23

1950 Bruce Brooks
1897 Marjorie Flack

*Is your current computer set up meeting your needs? What is lacking? How can you make it work for you?

> *"Fall seven times, stand up eight."*
> —Japanese Proverb

Tip: Your school's Web page should have a link to your library. Your link should include your mission statement, hours of operation, policy information, book lists for different grade levels, and good subject matter Web sites.

October 24 1907 Bruno Munari
1927 Barbara Robinson

> *"The bibliophile is the master of his books, the bibliomaniac their slave."*
> —*Hanns Bohatta*

October 25 1875 Carolyn Sherwin Bailey

> *"The final science is library science."*
> —*John Barth*

October 26
1941 Steven Kellogg
1934 Ellen Showell

*In order to improve communication with students, I plan to . . .

_____
_____
_____
_____
_____

> "Since new developments are the products of a creative mind, we must therefore stimulate and encourage that type of mind in every way possible."
> —George Washington Carver

Tip: Set aside time to meet regularly with your principal. At the beginning of the year, discuss his or her vision for the school and how you can help implement that vision. Share your vision for the library at this time. Later in the year, meet to discuss your progress in this area as well as sharing your thoughts for improvement in the library program. Near the end of the year, meet to discuss budget and program plans for the next year.

October 27
1889 Enid Bagnold
1924 Constance C. Greene

_____
_____
_____
_____
_____
_____
_____
_____

> "When we read a story, we inhabit it. The covers of the book are like a roof and four walls. What is to happen next will take place within the four walls of the story. And this is possible because the story's voice makes everything its own."
> —John Berger

Tip: Do it now. People will often say "Call me next week, and we'll set up a time then." Respond by saying, "Let's save ourselves a call and do it now."

Journal Pages *151*

October 28

*What is going to take a lot of hard work to change or fix in your work situation? What steps need to be taken before the problem is solved?

> "Opportunity is missed by most people because it is dressed in overalls and looks like work."
> —Thomas Alva Edison

___

October 29

> "Relativity teaches us the connection between the different descriptions of one and the same reality."
> —Albert Einstein

___

Tip: All of our library assistants are invited to join the Library Club. The Library Club meets once a month during our regular school activity period. Club meetings provide an opportunity for group training as well as friendship among the assistants.
—*Arlene Kachka, Head Librarian, Resurrection High School, Chicago, Illinois (Library Talk March/April 2002)*

October 30

> "Good as it is to inherit a library, it is better to collect one."
> —Augustine Birrell, **Book Buying** *(Obiter Dicta)*

Tip: To make the library media center feel more welcoming to everyone, replace "my" language with "our" language (i.e., our books, our OPAC terminals, our collection). This small change makes a big difference in how your customers view the library.

October 31

> "Shelved around us lie / The mummied authors."
> —Baynard Taylor, "Third Evening" **The Poet's Journal**

Tip: After each holiday, go to the party stores and pick up great decorations for 75% off. Next year when the holiday rolls around, you will be all set!

November

Ramadan usually begins in November, but can begin earlier. Ramadan is the Muslim month of purification by self-reflection, fasting from sunrise to sunset, peace making, and helping those in need.

Thanksgiving is the fourth Thursday of the month

"So dull and dark are the November days.
The lazy mist high up the evening curled,
And now the morn quite hides in smoke and haze;
The place we occupy seems all the world."
—*John Clare, November*

"November's sky is chill and drear,
November's leaf is red and sear."
—*Sir Walter Scott*

November 1
1935   Nicholosa Mohr
1902   Symeon Shimin

"It is vanity to persuade the world one hath much learning, by getting a great library."
—*Thomas Fuller*, The Holy and Profane States of Books. Maxim I.

Tip: Post citation information for Web sites next to your computers. Students will know while they are working what information they will need for their bibliographies.

November 2

"My history teacher was so old, he taught from memory."
—*Henny Youngman*

November 3   1908   Gyo Fujikawa

> *"She could give herself up to the written word as naturally as a good dancer to music or a fine swimmer to water. The only difficulty was that after finishing the last sentence she was left with a feeling at once hollow and uncomfortably full. Exactly like indigestion."*
> —Jean Rhys (1894–1979)

November 4   1906   Sterling North

*What piece of furniture would you most like to replace in this library? How would it change the library?

> *"Education helps you earn more. But not many schoolteachers can prove it."*
> —E. C. McKenzie

Tip: Sturdy couches and chairs can often be found inexpensively at thrift stores. Throw on a slipcover and you have a new reading nook!

November 5

> "Good teaching is one-fourth preparation and three-fourths theater."
> —Gail Godwin

November 6

> "What do we, as a nation, care about books? How much do you think we spend altogether on our libraries, public or private, as compared with what we spend on our horses?"
> —John Ruskin, Sesame and Lilies (Lect i, Of Kings' Treasuries)

November 7   1897   Armstrong Sperry

> *"Many hands make light work."*
> —*Unknown*

Tip: Set aside times to regularly meet with your paid staff as well as with volunteers. What is working for them? What changes would they like to see?

November 8   1932   Benjamin Bova
1945   Mariana Mayer
1847   Bram Stoker

> *"The medicine chest of the soul."*
> —*Inscription over the door of the Library at Thebes.*

November 9

Tip: Keep your staff informed about what is happening in the library. Each week send out an e-mail newsletter to the staff letting them know about upcoming events, new books in the collection, thank you to staff members or students, and other pertinent information. I even include a joke and trivia question each week with a prize for the correct answer—people will read it if there is a prize or a good joke buried in there!

November 10   1899   Kate Seredy

> "My books are very few, but then the world is before me — a library open to all — from which poverty of purse cannot exclude me — in which the meanest and most paltry volume is sure to furnish something to amuse, if not to instruct and improve."
> —Joseph Howe, Letter to George Johnson, January 1824.

November 11   Veterans Day

> "Education is simply the soul of a society as it passes from one generation to another."
> —G. K. Chesteron

November 12
1888   Anne Parrish
1928   Marjorie W. Sharmat

*What was you favorite novel as a child? What about this book touched you?

> "The student has his Rome, his Florence, his whole glowing Italy, within the four walls of his library. He has in his books the ruins of an antique world and the glories of a modern one."
> —Henry Wadsworth Longfellow (1807–1882)

Tip: I subscribe to Refdesk Link of the Day at <http://www.refdesk.com>. When I receive links that are interest to a particular teaching department or group of teachers, I forward the link to those teachers. It's an easy way to keep the library visible and helpful.
—Ellen Goldfinch, Peter Holt Memorial Library, Bishop's College School, Lennoxville, Quebec, Canada (Library Talk *May/June 2002*)

November 13 1915   Nathaniel Benchley
　　　　　　　　1850   Robert Louis Stevenson

*Why is important for you to take time to reflect each day? What lessons have you learned today?

> *"Reflection is what allows us to learn from our experiences: it is an assessment of where we have been and where we want to go next."*
> —Kenneth Wolf

_____

_____

_____

_____

_____

_____

_____

_____

November 14 1907   Astrid Lindgren
　　　　　　　　1899   Miska P.M. Mart Miles
　　　　　　　　1907   William Steig
　　　　　　　　1946   Nancy Tafuri

*What are you grateful for? How has being a librarian improved your life?

> *"There is a calmness to a life lived in gratitude, a quiet joy."*
> —Ralph H. Blum

_____

_____

_____

_____

_____

_____

_____

_____

November 15
- 1897 David McCord
- 1941 Daniel Manus Pinkwater

*If you were granted three wishes for your library, what would you wish for?

> "In seeking wisdom, the first step is silence, the second listening, the third remembering, the fourth practicing, the fifth—teaching others."
> —Ibn Gabirol, (c. 1022–1058)

Tip: Start a book discussion with other librarians. Have a theme each time you meet, and have everyone bring his or her top books for that theme. For example, one meeting might be science fiction; another time might be revolutionary war books. If everyone e-mails the bibliographic information to one person before the meeting, a complete handout of each theme can be assembled by just cutting and pasting from the e-mails onto a word document.

November 16
- 1947 Ann Blades
- 1915 Jean Fritz

> "You know the republic will survive when there is new money for libraries."
> —Denis Hamill

November 17

Tip: Since the magazine files may be visible to everyone, aesthetics really do matter. To solve the problem of ugly files, purchase pretty self stick wallpaper border in a width that covers the narrow shorter front of the file box. After washing the dust off the old boxes, apply the border to the fronts of the boxes. You may wish to decorate not only the boxes, but also the fronts of old file cabinets and the top fronts of bookcases that hold file boxes. The patterned border can tie old, disparately colored furnishings together for a lovely custom look.
—Jane Thompson, Ludlow (Massachusetts) High School (Library Talk *May/June 2001*)

November 18   1916   Sasek Miroslav

*What are three grant ideas you have that you would like to implement? Sometimes grant opportunities present themselves with a very fast turn around time. It is a good idea to have some ideas ready to pull out at a moment's notice.

> "I can shake off everything if I write. My sorrows disappear, my courage is reborn."
> —Anne Frank
>
> "The hardest thing to learn in life is which bridges to cross and which to burn."
> —David Russell

Tip: A great site for grants for schools is http://www.schoolgrants.org. It not only links you to sites that provide grants, but also gives you many good tips for writing grants.

November 19   1944   Patricia Polacco

*What makes you professionally "blush," metaphorically speaking?

> "Paper does not blush."
> —American Proverb

November 20   1919   William Cole

> "There are worse crimes than burning books. One of them is not reading them."
> —Joseph Brodsky

Tip: Teachers can be reluctant technology users and notoriously leery of change. We break this ice with "Two Minutes of Technology" at every faculty meeting, in which various teachers from different departments demonstrate a technology they're using. These presentations are brief, entertaining, real, and reassuring. On the agenda they're listed as "Brought to You by the Library", which gives us extra credibility, yet the only things we have to do are arrange for the presenters and introduce them.
—Kathy Fritts, Librarian, Jesuit High School, Portland, Oregon (Library Talk September/October 2002)

November 21
1908   Leo Politi
1908   Elizabeth George Speare

*If you could change one aspect of your job, what would you change?

> "Some students drink at the fountain of knowledge. Others just gargle."
> —E. C. McKenzie

November 22

*What is your favorite time of day at work?

> "Whether you believe you can do a thing or not, you are right."
> —Henry Ford

November 23

> *"The power of a text is different when it is read from when it is copied out. Only the copied text thus commands the soul of him who is occupied with it, whereas the mere reader never discovers the new aspects of his inner self that are opened by the text, that road cut through the interior jungle forever closing behind it: because the reader follows the movement of his mind in the free flight of day-dreaming, whereas the copier submits it to command."*
> —Walter Benjamin

November 24

- 1849 Frances H. Burnett
- 1826 Carlo Collodi
- 1933 Sylvia Engdahl
- 1921 Yoshika Uchida

> *"Whenever we improve the production, handling, and distribution of information we drop the price of thinking."*
> —Gregory J.E. Rawlins

November 25   1952   Crescent Dragonwagon
1909   Philip Eastman
1946   Marc Brown

*Which staff member is your biggest challenge? Why is this person a challenge? How can you change your attitude or behavior to more effectively deal with this person?

> *"It must be where the librarians hang out. Hey, let's get locked in here every weekend!"*
> —Arthur *episode, Line spoken by the character of Francine*

_____
_____
_____
_____
_____
_____
_____

November 26   1901   Doris Gates
1922   Charles Schulz

> *"Reading makes immigrants of us all. It takes us away from home, but more important, it finds homes for us everywhere."*
> —Hazel Rochman

_____
_____
_____
_____
_____

Tip: Even with an online cataloging provider, many free or reissued books that we receive are slow to make their way into the catalog. To provide a stopgap measure, we book marked our county-wide library system catalog. We look for an identical item or close match to the book in hand, pirate the Dewey number, and then add the first three letters of the author's last name instead of a cutter number. This method lets us get the books onto the shelves swiftly. Because these entries are all typed in caps, it's easy to upgrade them to full cataloging in batches as information becomes available for download.
—Sheryl Kindle Fullner, Nooksack Valley Middle School, Everson, Washington (**The Book Report** *September/October 2002*)

November 27

> "Nothing grieves a child more than to study the wrong lesson and learn something he wasn't suppose to."
> —E. C. McKenzie

November 28   1931   Tomi Ungerer

> "When a teacher calls a boy by his entire name, it means trouble."
> —Mark Twain

Tip: When you get a new item in the library, think of a staff member or a student who would like this item and check it out to them. Write them a quick note that you thought they would especially like this selection.

November 29

1832	Louisa May Alcott
1918	Madeleine L'Engle
1898	C. S. Lewis

> "She is too fond of books, and it has turned her brain."
> —Louisa May Alcott

November 30

1874	Lucy Maud Montogomery
1667	Jonathon Swift
1835	Mark Twain
1931	Margot Zemach

*What are you especially good at? How do you share your talent?

> "Imagine what a harmonious world it could be if every single person, both young and old, shared a little of what he is good at doing."
> —Quincy Jones

December

Hanukkah—Festival of Lights is this month

December 1   1949   Jan Brett

*Who is your favorite teacher at this school? What makes this person such a good teacher?

> "There is a brilliant child locked inside every student"
> —Marva Collins

December 2   1946   David Macaulay

> "Every library should try to be complete on something, if it were only the history of pinheads."
> —Oliver Wendell Holmes, The Poet at the Breakfast Table

Tip: Start a file for collecting quotes. This will come in handy when writing newsletters and memos.

Journal Pages 169

December 3

*What books calm you, refresh your soul?

> "Books are balm for the soul."
> —Donna Miller

December 4

Tip: Make a list of each type of bulb, ink cartridge, and other types of consumable items that need replacing from time to time and post the list on the door of the cabinet. Next to each item, note the number you have on hand. When you take an item out of the cabinet, cross off the current number and put the new number of stock on hand. As you get shipments, add the new items to the list. This way you will always have a current inventory at a glance and it will be easy to see what you are running low on and need to order.

December 5
 1910 Jim Kjelgaard
 1830 Christina Rossetti
 1933 Harve Zemach

*What is the biggest intellectual risk you have ever taken?

> "Teachers open the door, but you must enter by yourself."
> —Chinese Proverb

_____
_____
_____
_____
_____
_____
_____

Tip: Write your own professional mission statement. Then, when you have difficult decisions to make or problems to solve, revisit your mission statement before you proceed.

December 6 St. Nicholas Day
 1884 Cornelia Meigs
 1905 Elizabeth Yates

*What do you do to make sure your library "grows" the way you want it too?

> "Libraries are not made; they grow."
> —Augustine Birrell, Book Buying (Obiter Dicta)

_____
_____
_____
_____
_____
_____
_____

Tip: As you add new things to the library, it is also important to look at what can be discarded. It is not just books that need weeding. Do you have old, outdated AV equipment that should go? Broken chairs? Markers that don't work well? Get rid of them!

December 7 Pearl Harbor Day

*Who has been a bridge for you?

> "I am where I am because of the bridges that I crossed. Sojourner Truth was a bridge. Harriet Tubman was a bridge. Ida B. Wells was a bridge. Madame C. J. Walker was a bridge. Fannie Lou Hamer was a bridge."
> —Oprah Winfrey

Tip: Don't hoard supplies. A few paper clips soon become hundreds. Return surplus materials to the supply closet and free up space in your desk drawers.

December 8
1881   Padraic Colum
1894   James Thurber
1897   Edward Tunis

*What are some road blocks to success that you're experiencing? How can you create a way around these road blocks?

Tip: Purchase several $5 gift cards to the local movie theater to have on hand. When the custodian or someone else goes out of their way for you, this is a quick gift you can tuck into a thank you card.

December 9 1918 Jerome Beatty
　　　　　　　 1899 Jean de Brunhoff
　　　　　　　 1848 Joel Chandler Harris

*What books are on your holiday "to read" list?

> "It is well to read everything of something, and something of everything."
> —Lord Henry P. Brougham
> (1778–1868)

_____
_____
_____
_____
_____
_____

Tip: Before the winter holidays send a note home to parents with recommended magazines and subscribing information for the age group you work with. A magazine subscription insures that students will be reading year round.

December 10 1830 Emily Dickinson
　　　　　　　　1907 Rumer Godden
　　　　　　　　1903 Mary Norton
　　　　　　　　1879 Ernest Shepard

*What books feel like old friends to you? What books do you remember?

> "To read a book for the first time is to make an acquaintance with a new friend. To read it for a second time is to meet an old one. To read it for a third time means you have a very poor memory!"
> —Donna Miller

_____
_____
_____
_____
_____
_____

Tip: If you have a cabinet that hangs over a back room sink in your library, install cup hooks into the bottom of the cabinet. Hang clean cups from the hooks. This will save you time when you need to grab that quick cup of coffee and this is a great place to air dry the cups after you have washed them.

Journal Pages *173*

December 11

> "Classic: a book which people praise and don't read."
> —Mark Twain

Tip: When classes are waiting restlessly in line for their teachers to return, I grab a joke book and start reading. The kids quiet down, and my reluctant readers "discover" a book they want in the media center. This is an especially useful distraction during the holiday season.
—Pamela Gelbmann, Madison Elementary School, White Bear Lake, Minnesota (Library Talk November/December 2000)

December 12
1896 Ben Lucien Burman
1932 Barbara Emberly

> "If it is noticed that much of my outside work concerns itself with libraries, there is an extremely good reason for this. I think that the better part of my education, almost as important as that secured in the schools and the universities, came from libraries."
> —Irving Stone (1903–1989)

Tip: Hot wassail and holiday music in your library media center's workroom will provide a welcome respite for weary teachers and staff.

December 13
1916   Leonard Weisgard

*Is your library accessible to all patrons? Does the collection include characters who have different abilities? What can you do be more inclusive of all abilities?

> "The only disability in life is a bad attitude."
> —Scott Hamilton

Tip: Keep a copy of the ADA guidelines for libraries handy. It is full of specific recommendations for furniture, layout, and other building modifications. These facts and figures can come in very handy when writing grants to replace existing shelving, charge desks, or other remodeling needs.

December 14
1938   John Neufeld
1920   Rosemary Sutcliff

*To trust myself more I will . . . To learn to trust others more I will . . .

> "As soon as you trust yourself you will know how to live."
> —Johann Wolfgang Von Goethe

Tip: To help find books that students have checked out and misplaced, make a wanted poster telling students that the following books have "Escaped from the Library." Offer a reward for their return. List all the titles and call numbers of "escaped" books. The students who checked the books out are still responsible for them, but usually those students are the ones who later find the books. (You may not want to give a reward to the student who originally misplaced the book!)
—*Judy Wolbert, North Clarion (Pennsylvania) Elementary (Library Talk May/June 2002)*

December 15   1896   Ann Nolan Clark

*What have you been procrastinating about lately? How can you move to action?

> *"God has promised forgiveness to your repentance; but God has not promised tomorrow to your procrastination."*
> —*Saint Augustine*

Tip: Consider thanking all the people who use your media center by having an appreciation week for teachers, students, or administrators. The week could include serving snacks at an informal social, showcasing the different services your media center offers, and showcasing and previewing library materials. You could offer small tokens such as bookmarks, pens, or water bottles. This is your way of making your patrons feel special and encouraging new patrons to see what the media center is all about. Be sure to advertise this event with bright, colorful flyers or daily announcements, or make a commercial promoting the event during announcements or Channel One time.
—*Mercedes Smith, Bishop Kennedy High School, Jacksonville, Florida (Library Talk May/June 2002)*

December 16   1932   Quentin Blake
1917   Arthur C. Clarke
1927   Peter Dickinson
1893   Marie Hall Ets

December 17

Tip: To solicit funds for purchasing new books for the library media center, decorate your library's holiday tree, by hanging paper "books" on the tree upon which you have written the titles of books that are needed for the library's collection. Put up a sign that reads "Give a gift to your library media center."

December 18
1927 Marilyn Sachs
1884 Alison Uttley

"Writing teaches us our mysteries."
—Marie De L'Incarnation

December 19
1928 Eve Bunting
1868 Eleanor H. Porter

*Is there a student you think would be a good librarian some day? What qualities does this student possess that would help him or her become successful in this field? What can you do to encourage this person to consider that library field?

> "The only educational aspect of television is that it puts the repair man's kids through college."
> —Joan Welsh

December 20
1892 Richard Atwater
1940 M. B. Goffstein

> "The media program provides a bridge between formal, school-based learning and independent, lifelong learning,"
> —Barbara Barnard Stein and Celia Burger, "A Community for Learning," Teacher Librarian

December 21

Tip: We focus on our student's visual arts talent by showcasing an "Artist of the Week" throughout the school year. The art teacher chooses an outstanding creation from each week's work to display in the front window of our library. She loaned me an easel for displaying paintings, drawings, ...and we have a small table for sculpture. I add a note that provides the artist's name, the title of the work, and the medium in which it was created. During Monday morning announcements, we announce the name of that week's artist and the title of the chosen work. I make a certificate for the student whose work is shown, thanking them for sharing their talent and making our library a more beautiful place. I put a "smiley" face sticker on the certificate and present it to the students with a candy treat. To publicize our local talent, I wrote a brief article for our local newspaper describing the program and included a picture of several of the students whose work had been shown.
—*Julia Steger, Librarian, Clifton Middle School, Covington, Virginia* (Library Talk *September/October 2002)*

December 22   1917   William O. Steele

*Truly leave work behind and just write about the magical holiday moments that are occurring for you.

December 23
	1937	Avi
	1950	Erick Ingraham

*Watch an old holiday movie. Write about the impact this movie had on your life in an earlier time.

> "There's a period of life when we swallow a knowledge of ourselves, and it becomes either good or sour inside."
> —Pearl Bailey

December 24
	1891	Feodor Rojankovsky
	1920	Noel Streatfield

> "It is not the eye that sees the beauty of the heavens, nor the ear that hears the sweetness of music, but the soul."
> —Jeremy Taylor

December 25   Christmas Day
    1869   Charles J. Finger
    1880   Johnny Gruelle

*What was the best gift you ever gave someone?

> *"Happy, happy Christmas, that can win us back to the delusions of our childhood days, recall to the old man the pleasures of his youth, and transport the traveler back to his own fireside and quiet home!"*
> —Charles Dickens

December 26   Kwanzaa begins today
Boxing Day
    1937   Jan Van Leeuwen
    1867   Ella Young

> *"The way you bring up a child is the way it grows up."*
> —Swahili proverb

December 27   1904   Ingri Parin D'Aulaire

*If this holiday season has provided a sense of comfort for you, how can you carry that feeling over into the new year and into your work life?

> *"Knowledge exists to be imparted."*
> —*Ralph Waldo Emerson*

December 28   1895   Carol Ryrie Brink
1919   Emily Neville

> *"Go to your bosom, knock there, and ask what your heart doth know."*
> —*William Shakespeare*

December 29   1943   Molly Bang
　　　　　　　　1925   E.W. Hildick

> "I do not teach, I relate."
> —Montaigne

Tip: Keep used tissue paper from packages. This can be used for a variety of things from placing pieces between photos when storing them to making paper flowers for decorating bulletin boards.

December 30   1856   Rudyard Kipling
　　　　　　　　1943   Mercer Mayer

> "The one who knows others is wise. The one who knows oneself is enlightened."
> —Lao-Tzu

Tip: Set aside time every day to deal with phone calls, letters, and bills. This should not be much more than half an hour. You may not need that much time every day but it is better to be safe than leave these things to their own devices. Schedule this time in your plan book so it is there if you need it.

December 31   1906   Pamela Bianco

*Looking at the past year, what were your greatest accomplishments? How can you build on those successes?

> "Even people who sleep in the same bed dream their own dreams."
> —Chinese Proverb

Tip: Purchase a small toolbox with tools. Label each tool "Library." Also have on hand a variety of sizes of nuts, bolts, and nails. This way small repairs can be handled immediately before they turn into large problems.

Bibliography

Miller, James E. *The Rewarding Practice of Journal Writing: A Guide for Starting and Keeping Your Personal Journal.* Fort Wayne, IN: Willowgreen, 1998.

Rainer, Tristine. *The New Diary: How to Use a Journal for Self Guidance and Expanded Creativity.* New York: Jeremy P. Tarcher/Putnam, 1978.

Woodard, Patricia. *Journal Jumpstarts: Quick Topics and Tips for Journal Writing.* Fort Collins, CO: Cottonwood, 1994.

Yucht, Alice. Personal interview. 14 Nov. 2002.

For Further Reading

Books

Dillard, Annie. *The Writing Life.* New York: Harper, 1999.

Lamott, Anne. *Bird by Bird: Some Instructions on Writing and Life.* New York: Knopf, 1995.

Rico, Gabriele. *Writing the Natural Way: Turn the Task of Writing into the Joy of Writing.* New York: Putnam, 2000.

Web sites

HolidayOrganizers.com: Gifts in a Jar: Journal Jar by Cynthia Townley Ewer, Editor, OrganizedHome.Com <http://holidayorganizer.com/gifts/giftsjar/journal.html>

The Journal: The Premiere Journaling Software by David Michael, 2002 <http://www.davidrm.com/thejournal/newsletter/tjnews02-05.html>

Professional Reflective Journaling by Patricia E. Eagle, 1999–2001 <http://home.earthlink.net/~peeagle/benefits.html>

About the Authors

Donna Miller is currently the Editor for Linworth Publishing, Inc. Donna was an educator for over 25 years as a band director, library media specialist, and district administrator. Donna has also served as a school library consultant throughout the state of Texas and in Colorado and an adjunct professor for Texas Woman's University. She holds a Master's Degree in Music Education from Texas Woman's University and in Library Science from the University of North Texas. Donna's professional accomplishments include membership in Beta Phi Mu Honor Society, Who's Who in American Education 1996/1997, and the Colorado Library Advisory Board. Donna has been an author, reviewer, and columnist for Linworth Publishing for many years and co-authored with J'Lynn Anderson the Linworth book *Developing an Integrated Library Program*. Donna resides in Grand Junction, Colorado with her husband JD and two border collies Dakota and SAM.

Karen Larsen has been a classroom teacher and a library media specialist for over 20 years. She holds one Master's degree in Information Technology: School Library Media and another Master's degree in Talented and Gifted Education. She was named the 2002 National Gifted and Talented Teacher of the Year by the National Association for Gifted Children. This is her third book. Her other titles include: *Careers!* published by ALPS publications (http://www.alpspublishing.com/) and *State by State, Step by Step*—a guide for studying the states by Pieces of Learning <http://www.piecesoflearning.com/>. Both books are hands-on, standards based units that can be used by classroom teachers or collaboratively taught with the school library media specialist. Karen lives in Westminster, Colorado with her daughters, Kyla and Brenna, and her husband, Brian.

www.ingramcontent.com/pod-product-compliance
Lightning Source LLC
Chambersburg PA
CBHW080539300426
44111CB00017B/2799